POETRY
WALES
25
YEARS

POETRY WALES

25

YEARS

Edited by
Cary Archard

SEREN BOOKS

SEREN BOOKS is the book imprint of
Poetry Wales Press Ltd
Andmar House, Tondu Road,
Bridgend, Mid Glamorgan

The Selection and Introduction © Cary Archard, 1990
The Texts © the authors

ISBN 1-85411-031-4

*The publisher acknowledges the financial support of the
Welsh Arts Council*

Typeset in 10½ point Plantin
Printed by Billings, Worcester

CONTENTS

Introduction

When Meic Stephens published the first issue of *Poetry Wales* in the spring of 1965, he was responding with characteristic vision and energy to the desperate shortage of outlets in Wales for English Language writers. That first year, two slim numbers were produced, soon there were three a year and by 1970 the magazine had become the regular quarterly Wales now takes for granted. The sceptics who originally questioned the need for a magazine devoted solely to poetry have long been silenced. As any of the six editors would testify, there has never been a shortage of material, indeed, the problem has nearly always been what to leave out.

For twenty-five years, for most of which it has enjoyed the warm support of the Welsh Arts Council, the magazine's purpose has remained constant: to encourage poets in Wales by printing their poetry and reviewing their books, to inform English readers about poetry in the Welsh language, and to place the poetry of Wales in a broader international context. As the correspondence section has demonstrated, there has always been a cutting edge to the magazine. It has been unashamedly nationalist and political without being inward-looking or myopic. (Some of the more important issues are discussed in the lively editorials included in this selection.) The magazine's aim has been so large and so much has appeared between its covers that making this anthology has been an almost impossible task. The final selection is bound to seem somewhat arbitrary when the editor is forced to reduce some 10,000 items from 94 separate issues to one book.

Because of space, there are some things the reader won't find here. All reviews have been excluded and it has only been possible to include a tiny fraction of the dozens of critical articles for which the magazine has become so well-known. The highly-praised special issues, on writers such as the three Thomases, R.S., Dylan, and Edward, on David Jones, Idris Davies, Dafydd ap Gwilym, T.H. Parry-Williams and Alun Lewis, are barely represented at all. As most of these issues are unobtainable, it is hoped that these striking omissions will be rectified in the future by at least two further books, one devoted to critical essays and another to the

9

articles on and about the Welsh language, another area very thinly represented here.

This anthology, then, concentrates on the poetry and on the poets. Almost ninety writers are included in its 250 pages. The editor chose items primarily because he enjoyed them. It wasn't his intention to represent different periods or different editors' tastes, yet a policy emerged during the selecting. However much the editor enjoyed a particular writer's work, he set a limit of two, or at most, three, of that individual's items being included. Nearly all the writers from outside Wales have been deliberately overlooked in favour of the homegrown product. Poets who have appeared relatively often in the magazine are more likely to be found in these pages than those who were published infrequently.

While making his choice this editor has been very aware of the debt he owes to the editorial decisions of the other editors of *Poetry Wales*: to Gerald Morgan (3 issues), Sam Adams (8), Mike Jenkins (16 so far), J.P. Ward (20) and Meic Stephens, the founder (23). That there were so many good things to choose from is a tribute to each one's consistent judgement and remarkable energy. The material has been arranged chronologically and an effort made to fairly represent, in the number of allocated pages, each editor's period at the magazine.

Perhaps this anthology will remind regular *Poetry Wales* readers of the interesting items they have forgotten, perhaps it will surprise them. If new readers so enjoy what they find here that they subscribe to the magazine, making the selection will have been worthwhile.

CARY ARCHARD

HERBERT WILLIAMS

Depopulation

They say this is no place for the ambitious.
The young men leave, trailing
A pity for the people left behind,
Nailing the coffin of the town they go,
Finding refreshment in familiar lies.

Far from the accustomed hills, they build
The structure of success which they were told
Would monument their paragon advance,
If only they were bold enough to leave
The moment they were old enough to go.

So now this is no place for the ambitious.
With every decade it is more
Conclusively a place which people leave
The moment they are bold enough to go.

Some have no regrets. But others find
A virtue in the ruin left behind,
And long to verify the truths
Their fathers read, and tread
The ways that scored their rooted enterprise,
And nurture a simplicity, until
A darkness comes to cover up their eyes.

But ambitious they are, ambitious to a man,
Made ambitious by their education,
Prisoners of their nourished talents.

So they display the customary
Pity for the people left behind.
But their bleak hearts speak
The bitter language of the dispossessed.

ROBERT MORGAN

Blood Donor

The searching was easy and memory ripens
On the grey earth picture of Rees
In his grimy vest soaked in blood.
Forty-eight years under tense rock
Had stripped him like a naked tree with roots
In slag and marked him with texture of strain
And accident. But it was slow legs
And dust-worn eyes that were to blame.

The iron rock-bar was still in his hands
Held like a spear of a fallen warrior.
The rocks had dyed his silver hair red
And the heavy bar was warm and worn.
Blind flies swarmed in the blood-sweat
Air and the tough men with bruised
Senses were gentle, using distorted
Hands like women arranging flowers.

On the way out, through twisting roads of rocky
Silence, you could sense images of confusion
In the slack chain of shadows; muscles
Were nerve-tight and thoughts infested
With wrath and sharp edges of fear.
Towards the sun's lamp we moved, taking
Home the dark prisoner in his shroud of coats.

ALUN REES

Release John Lucifer!

It's time they let the devil out of hell.
Remember how they threw him in the cell
and tossed away the key? And all because
he figured he could run the business well,
perhaps a little better than the boss.

This was the boy most likely to succeed.
"This is the kind of fellow that we need,"
imagine heavenly civil servants saying.
But not the sort they wanted in the lead.
Yet even Pilate granted Christ a hearing.

Take-over bids for heaven happen once.
Angelic cops don't give a second chance.
The company directors called a squad
to clear the meeting. They were late for lunch,
and they were getting hungry. So was God.

MEIC STEPHENS

Ponies, Twynyrodyn

Winter, the old drover, has brought
these beasts from the high moor's hafod
to bide the bitter spell among us,
here, in the valley streets.
Observe them, this chill morning, as
they stand, backsides against the wind,
in Trevithick Row. Hoofs, shod with ice,
shift and clatter on the stone kerb.
Steam is slavering from red nostrils,
manes are stiff with frost and dung.

Quiet now, last night
they gallivanted through the village,
fear's bit in teeth. Hedges were broken,
there was havoc to parked cars. Yet,
despite the borough council's by-laws
these refugees are welcome here.
Fed from kitchen and tommybox, they
are free to roam the grit backlanes,
only kids and mongrels pester them.
We greet them as old acquaintances
not because they bring us local colour,
as the tourist guides might say, but
for the brute glamour that is with them.
Long before fences and tarmac, they
were the first tenants of these valleys,
their right to be here is freehold.
Now, in this turncoat weather, as
they lord it through the long terraces,
toppling bins from wet steps, ribs
rubbing against the bent railings,
our smooth blood is disturbed
by hiraeth for the lost cantrefi,
the green parishes that lie beyond
the borders of our town and hearts,
fit for nothing now but sad songs.
These beasts are our companions,
dark presences from the peasant past,
these grim valleys our common hendre,
exiles all, until the coming thaw.

DAVID GWENALLT JONES

The Dead

With his fiftieth birthday behind him, a man sees with fair clarity
    The people and surroundings that made him what he is,
And the steel ropes that tether me strongest to these things,
    In a village of the South, are the graves in two cemeteries.

I'd ride a bike pilfered from scrap, or with a pig's bladder
    Play rugby for Wales; and all that while,
Little thought I'd hear how two of my contemporaries
    Would spew into a bucket their lungs red and vile.

Our neighbours they were, a family from Merthyr Tydfil,
    The 'martyrs' we called them, by way of a pun,
And five of them, by turns, had a cough that crossed the fences
    To break up our chatter and darken all our fun.

We crept in the Bibled parlours, and peeped with awe
    At cinders of flesh in the coffin, and ashes of song,
And there we learnt, over lids screwed down before their time,
    Collects of red revolt and litanies of wrong.

Not the death that goes his natural rounds, like a gaol warder,
    Giving notice in the clink of his damp keys,
But the leopard of industry leaping sudden and sly
    That strikes from fire and water men to their knees.

The hootering death: the dusty, smokefull, drunken death,
    Death whose dreadful grey destiny was ours;
Explosion and flood changed us often into savages
    Fighting catastrophic and devilish powers.

Mute and brave women with a fistful of blood money,
    With a bucketful of death, forever the rankling of loss,
Carrying coal, chopping wood for a fire, or setting the garden
    And more and more reading the Passion of the Cross.

This Sunday of Flowers, as we place on their grave a bunch
    Of silicotic roses and lilies pale as gas,
Between the premature stones and the curb yet unripened,
    We gather the old blasphemings, curses of funerals past.

Our Utopia vanished from the top of Gellionnen,
    Our abstract humanity's classless, defrontiered reign,
And today nothing is left at the deep root of the mind
    Save family and neighbourhood, man's sacrifice and pain.

Translated from the Welsh by Anthony Conran.

HARRI WEBB

Thanks In Winter

The day that Eliot died, I stood
By Dafydd's grave in Ystrad Fflur.
It was the depth of winter,
A day for an old man to die.
The dark memorial stone,
Chiselled in marble of Latin
And the soft intricate gold
Of the old language,
Echoed the weather's colour
A slate vault over Ffair Rhos,
Pontrhydfendigaid, Pumlumon,
The sheep runs, the rough pasture
And the lonely whitewashed houses
Scattered like frost, the dwellings
Of country poets, last inheritors
To the prince of song who lies
Among princes, among ruins.
A pilgrim under the yew at Ystrad Fflur
I kept my vow, prayed for my country,
Cursed England, came away

And home to the gas fire and television
News. Caught between two languages,
Both dying, I thanked the long-dead
Minstrel of May and the newly silent
Voice of the bad weather, the precise
Accent of our own time, taught
To the disinherited, offering
Iron for gold.

VERNON WATKINS

Swallows

Artists are swallows
Building a nesting-place of earth.
The far each follows,
Returning always to his place of birth.

Welsh ambassadors,
Stubborn of instinct, mould in clay
The travelled shores,
And break down colours from an earlier day.

Vision lifts the mind,
Turning their swallows' flight to grace.
In eaves they find,
But nowhere on the ground, a settled place.

Linked in heart and cry,
They weave a lost age. Devious wings
Trace in crossed sky
A timeless writing, strict as tightened strings.

Bow and harpstring both
Sound where a seawave hits the sand.
Eager and loth,
The two vibrations answer the one hand.

Savage history throws
Chance to the winds and cuts the thread.
Iron and rose
Point recollection, trim the arrowhead.

Here Aneirin drew
Anguish from stone for youth cut down.
Here Llywarch threw
Remorse at Death, who took his every son.

Thought and arrow once
Flew from the rockhead's ambush. Now
Those fallen sons
Haunt the bleak furrows, interrupt the plough.

Still Taliesin stays,
Touching, more near than all we know,
The pulse of praise,
Deeper, more strong, than string of harp or bow.

Sword and rattling shield
Tell, in plucked verse, how sharp-edged war
Struck, in the field.
Without Christ's birth how vain Earth's mornings are.

These, whose flight is toil,
Live but to praise the elusive mark;
Whether in oil,
Sculpture, verse, music, keen wings cut through dark.

Storm will but restore
The wings' true balance. Faith can make
Love's metaphor
Strong, to give time more truth, the more time take.

EMYR HUMPHREYS

Ancestors

One

The dead are horizontal and motionless
They take less room
Than the stones which mark the tomb

But the words they spoke
Grow like flowers in the cracked rock

Their ghosts move easily between words
As people move between trees
Gathering days and sunlight
Like fuel for an invisible fire.

Two

Grandparents whose portraits hang
Like ikons in our hearts
Carved out acres drew up codicils
To brace our lives
But the new estates cover the fields
All the names are changed and their will
Is broken up by sewers and pylons.

Three

Our remote ancestors knew better.
They were all poets
They all wove
Syllabic love into their wooden homes.

They saw the first invaders come
Pushing their boats through the water meadows

Their teeth and their swords glittering in the
   stealthy light
And they carved metrical systems out of their
   own flesh.

Four

The air is still committed to their speech
Their voices live in the air
Like leaves like clouds like rain
Their words call out to be spoken
Until the language dies
Until the ocean changes.

MEIC STEPHENS

The Second Flowering

Now that my connection as publisher and editor of *Poetry
Wales* has been severed, it has been suggested by the new editor,
Mr. Gerald Morgan, that this may be an appropriate moment to
record the circumstances in which I launched the magazine three
years ago. Like Bryn Griffiths in the Dent anthology *Welsh Voices*
published last summer, he has been kind enough to claim that my
magazine has played a major part in fostering the younger
generation of Anglo-Welsh poets and believes that the publication of its first seven numbers should be chronicled now. I gladly
accept Gerald Morgan's invitation, after a suitable blush, because
it offers such a splendid opportunity of exercising my critical
faculties, so long cramped in the editorial chair.

When I was about to bring out the first number of *Poetry
Wales* in the spring of 1965, I knew perhaps a dozen young poets
who, in one way or another, might have been dubbed Anglo-
Welsh. Only three had volumes to their names and the only
magazines that published their work were *The London Welshman* and *The Anglo-Welsh Review*, both of which had other

responsibilities and were based in England. Indeed, most of the poets I had read were living in England at that time and contributing to English literary reviews. It seemed that the brilliance of *Wales*, whose brief revival had dazzled my undergraduate years, was snuffed out forever. Of the older generation, David Jones was known only to a select few, Vernon Watkins and R.S. Thomas were established abroad but begrudged at home, and hardly a hair was turned when T.H. Jones, whose three volumes were almost unknown among his own people, was drowned in Australia. The only new voice in the Anglo-Welsh wilderness was Anthony Conran's, with his masterly essays in *The Anglo-Welsh Review* and his privately circulated pamphlets of verse, but even he was yet to realise the promise of his *Formal Poems* (1960) or to publish his distinguished translations from the Welsh.

Then, even as I was busy correcting proofs for the first number of *Poetry Wales*, there appeared in the London Welsh St. David's Day programme an impassioned plea by Professor Gwyn Jones, former editor of *The Welsh Review,* for a new Anglo-Welsh magazine. "That there is no new or better *Wales* or *Welsh Review* appearing in Wales today is inexcusable. That there is no little magazine which would allow us to see and sift the poets is shocking. The best thing that could happen to Anglo-Welsh letters just now would be the emergence of some piercingly bright and original talent. The second best thing would be the appearance of an exciting but authoritative journal which would give young creative writers their chance but not cosset them. The first of these desiderata would be an Act of God; but the second is quickly compassable by any man worth his salt. The difficulties are many, and the problems complex — but then they always were. In a rough and ready way writers get the journals they deserve. Is there no Welshman now breathing who can provide one? His rewards would be tremendous, a forum for views, a platform for talent, and maybe a launching pad for genius. In the mid-sixties I think Anglo-Welsh literature could move off with all the *élan* of thirty years ago, and not as a copy of the past but something golden, new-minted. There is plenty of paper, plenty of ink, plenty of writers. Who will bring them together and give Wales what she needs?" Well, there was a challenge not to be ignored; so, never much impressed by my own muse, I pressed on with high hopes as an editor.

My intention, at least in those early months, was to satisfy a personal preoccupation with the psychology of English-speaking Welshmen, particularly the writers, by enquiring how much and what standard of verse was being written in English about Wales. I came to my task with no real knowledge of the Welsh language or its literature, but with an interest that had first flickered when, as a boy at school, I had read every title in the Local Authors section of Pontypridd public library. I was also a member of Plaid Cymru committed to the nationalist cause in Merthyr Tydfil and regarded my literary interest as a pleasant, perhaps complementary, diversion from the political dog-fight. Looking back, I must admit that it was difficult to separate my literary motives from my political, perhaps because I was then too much impressed by Irish and French precedents; but I will not apologise for that. I was content to make my magazine "unashamedly about the parish of Wales", as Raymond Garlick once described it in a letter to me.

The first number of *Poetry Wales*, with its black Arianrhod a proud if baffling figure on the cover, appeared in April, 1965. With the recent failure of *Welsh Outlook* in mind, I was steeled against watching my magazine suffer the same fate as so many English-language periodicals in Wales, guttering after a few numbers. So nobody was more surprised than the editor when the first number, carrying twenty poems by sixteen poets, received a warm welcome everywhere and sold five hundred copies within a month. If you happen to own a copy, by the way, don't let the baby chew it because it's fetching twenty-five shillings on the American market.

The spadework was mostly mine, of course, but Ruth, my wife, handled the business side and kept a *croeso* for the poets who trooped to our home every weekend. I was also encouraged by the enthusiasm of two good friends, Harri Webb and Gerald Morgan, with whom I had discussed the need for an Anglo-Welsh magazine. Keidrych Rhys, who as editor of the legendary *Wales* was mainly responsible for the first flowering of Anglo-Welsh verse in the nineteen forties, sent valuable advice. Good wishes arrived from A.G. Prys-Jones, editor of the first Anglo-Welsh anthology in 1917, from Roland Mathias, editor of *The Anglo-Welsh Review,* and from Raymond Garlick, its first editor, from his exile in Holland. Poems and reviews came from established poets like Glyn Jones, R.S. Thomas and Dannie Abse. From Vernon Watkins, that kind man and dedicated poet whose death has been announced this week, I received several letters of encouragement. (Surely it would be appropriate, now that he has gone, to endow a major poetry prize in Wales and name it after him?) Then, with our removal to Cardiff in the autumn of 1966, I was glad to make the acquaintance of John Stuart Williams, Cyril Hodges and Herbert Williams. To Cyril Hodges, in particular, I would like to record here my gratitude for his generous patronage. Meanwhile, in London, *Poetry Wales* was being sold by new poets like John Tripp, Sally Roberts (Jones), Leslie Norris, Tom Earley and Robert Morgan, all members of the Guild of Welsh Writers which, by a happy coincidence, had been founded in the same spring as my magazine. Its chairman and leading light was Bryn Griffiths who became not only a catalyst for the new group but the best publicity man that any magazine in Wales has ever had in the former capital. So that, by the end of our second year, *Poetry Wales* had a hundred subscribers, the Welsh Committee of the Arts Council had granted financial assistance, the magazine had taken its place on counters all over Wales, in Dublin, London, Paris, in many libraries in the United States, and most important of all, Anglo-Welsh poets at last seemed to be as numerous as blackberries in the woods. To those already mentioned I would add the names of Peter Gruffydd, Alison Bielski, Alun Rees, David John Lines, Peter Preece, John Idris Jones, Douglas Phillips, Bruton Connors and John Ormond. All these became contributors to *Poetry Wales* and it is chiefly about them we must speak when we consider the second flowering of Anglo-Welsh verse since the world war.

Let me begin with a grouse about the Dent anthology that Bryn Griffiths edited this year. No doubt his introductory remark that "it has proved impossible to include all the poets or all the poems" was meant to disarm the inevitable criticism that the book is by no means representative of the new Anglo-Welsh generation. But it fails to convince me because, a line later, the editor claims that "the poems I have chosen, however, seem to me representative of the best work written by Anglo-Welsh poets during the last twenty years". It is here that I cannot agree with Bryn Griffiths. Of the thirty poets mentioned above, new and established, no less than nineteen are included in *Welsh Voices* and, given the editor's brief which was dictated by the publisher's costs, no more could be expected, although such omissions as John Ormond and Alison Bielski among the living, and T.H. Jones among the dead, are to be queried. But it is with the choice of poems that I am not at all happy and cannot help but agree with those who have found the book disappointing in its standards. For it seems to me that Bryn Griffiths set about his task in a confused way and failed to carry out the preliminary, so necessary to the anthologist, of reading *all* the poems of each poet before making his selection. Instead, it seems he asked each poet to send a maximum of ten poems and chose from among those, without specifying whether the poems should be new or already published. He also picked what he liked from periodicals and volumes that he happened to see. Thus R.S. Thomas has three poems from his books, including the old favourites 'Welsh Landscape' and 'Iago Prytherch', and five unpublished ones. Of the seventy-eight poems in the anthology, eighteen and nearly one quarter had previously appeared in *Poetry Wales* and most of the rest in various periodicals during the last three years. Hence, for example, the distortion of Raymond Garlick's work: 'Still Life', a brand new but unexceptional poem, and 'Saunders Lewis at Newtown', already published in *Poetry Wales* under the title 'The Cymrodorion Lecture'; that's all, nothing from Raymond Garlick's volumes which, of course, contain his most outstanding poems. Again, the quantitative representation of the poets tends to mislead. Raymond Garlick and Glyn Jones, for example, are by general assent among the most distinguished Anglo-Welsh poets, yet they have only two poems each here, while Robert Morgan and Sally Roberts (Jones), for example, young poets with no volumes to their names, have six and seven poems each; while Anthony Conran, surely the most prolific of all during the last ten years, has four poems here which first appeared in the college magazine at Bangor in 1957.

Perhaps I have said enough to suggest, kindly I hope, that Bryn Griffiths should have taken the precaution of clarifying his selection principles or at least, offered us a more substantial introduction. To argue that *Welsh Voices* is no more than a personal choice and that anyone is free to bring out another simply will not do, because the book has queered the pitch and it seems unlikely now that any major publisher with world-wide distribution facilities will be prepared to bring out another anthology of contemporary Anglo-Welsh verse for a few years yet. This should not prevent any Welsh publisher from tackling the job, however. We have waited patiently since the publication of the Faber anthology that Keidrych Rhys edited in 1944. The need in 1967 was not for one man's personal choice from the work of living poets, which was bound to be disputable, but for a balanced, thoroughly informed and authoritative selection that would do for Anglo-Welsh literature the service of presenting, to our own countrymen and to the world, the best poems by all the poets who have contributed since the war. A sociological introduction and a critical assessment would lend such a work the impact that Anthony Conran brought to his *Penguin Book of Welsh Verse*. In recent years, several anthologies have put Scottish and Irish literature on the world map but, in Wales, the anthology that will be to Anglo-Welsh literature what Thomas Parry's Oxford Book is to Welsh literature is still to be compiled. I can only hope that Gerald Morgan's *This World of Wales*, to be published soon by the University of Wales Press, and Glyn Jones' appraisal of Anglo-Welsh writers, planned by Dent for next spring, will compensate and point the way.

I am aware that my argument begs the question: are there enough Anglo-Welsh poets writing well today to justify such a serious approach? By my reckoning there are about thirty, with newcomers showing considerable promise all the time. I think that is a respectable batch; there were thirty-seven in the Faber anthology edited by Keidrych Rhys and just about everyone was represented there. Perhaps there have never been more at any one time. I discount those listed before the present century because it is my opinion that Anglo-Welsh literature is a recent phenomenon. It has its roots in newly disturbed soil — the social and linguistic upheaval that occurred in Wales during the inter-war years. Perhaps I should add that if there is an Anglo-Welsh tradition three hundred years old, as Raymond Garlick has so attractively argued, it certainly does not mean much to most of the poets in this century. Quite frankly, there seems to be something rather over-compensatory in seeking to find an Anglo-Welsh tradition among the tourists, anglicised gentry, and country parsons who dabbled in English verse from Tudor times on. But that is not to say that those poets who made their names during the years 1930-1960 and the new men about us now have not done a great deal to lay the foundations of a tradition that is likely to last, even after Welsh self-government, well into the next century. I am not looking for a school or a movement, because that presupposes a common manifesto. Only this much is clear: the new poets, with one or two lone wolves to remind us that labels in poetry are so often phoney, all recognise that they have a great deal in common, including a social background, roots if you like in a particular community. They are also willing to associate as Welshmen and have their work discussed with reference to the culture of Wales. I do not think the same could be said for the generation of Alun Lewis or Dylan Thomas, for all his posturing.

The reason, I am sure, has to do with the growth of national consciousness that has taken place in Wales since the war. It is significant that most of the poets, like their compatriots who write in Welsh, support the nationalist cause, while several are politically committed and almost all take an interest in Welsh affairs. That is why I could not help but make *Poetry Wales* a nationalist publication and why political questions must be asked in any consideration of Anglo-Welsh verse these days. The influence of R.S. Thomas is, of course, much in evidence here but his brooding on rural decay and the spineless attitudes of his countrymen may well prove to be an emotional dead-end, however salutary for the time being. The new poets, it seems to me, are not so much concerned with 'things as they are', although the occasional poem is still in their repertoire, as with seeking a creative way out of the present impasse. Poets like Raymond Garlick, Harri Webb and John Tripp, have made their vision of a free Wales the theme for poems that I consider to be among the finest written about this country. I am not suggesting that all Anglo-Welsh poets should feel obliged to write about Welsh nationhood, but I am convinced that before a poet writing in English can fully justify his position as Anglo-Welsh, he needs either to write about Welsh scenes, Welsh people, the Welsh past, life in contemporary Wales, or his own analysis of all these, or else attempt to demonstrate in his verse those more elusive characteristics of style and feeling which are generally regarded as belonging to Welsh poetry. We are in desperate need of a good critic who will define the Welshness of Anglo-Welsh verse and it seems to me that such matters will have to be properly discussed soon if our poets are to receive the critical attention they merit.

The big danger threatening Anglo-Welsh verse, as I see it, is that it is and may continue to be peripheral, both in Wales and in England. It worries me to see so many, about a third, of the leading poets resident in England. There is no good reason, except "the whistle of the English pound", to keep Welshmen in London and the English provinces these days and I insist that poets should be the first to live among the people and the scenes they praise, lest all suffer. While so many of us acquiesce in the anglo-centric organisation of life in Britain today, I think our literature will remain in much the same position as Scotland's before its renaissance in the nineteen twenties: parochial, disorientated, minor, conservative, dull, and without one poet, or a critic, of Hugh Macdiarmid's stature. Like him, our poets must strive "to break their living tomb". Whether we are likely to flourish and create a literature that measures up to European standards is not yet clear. The only alternative, for me, is that, with the Welsh nation denied the rights and responsibilities of full nationhood, a parliament at least, and therefore obliterated by the end of the present century, the Welsh will have completely lost their separate identity and the Anglo-Welsh will have nothing to distinguish them from other regional English writers.

Meanwhile, it seems to me a reasonable safeguard against such an appalling disaster to attempt a *rapprochement* between those whose creative work is done in Welsh and the Anglo-Welsh. There has long been sympathy in both camps, but hopefully the most recent initiative has been shown by the Welsh speakers themselves, notably by such eminent Welshmen as Aneirin Talfan Davies and Professor Jac L. Williams who have argued on behalf of the Anglo-Welsh in Welsh journals. Only the dinosaurs have refused to listen and they, mercifully, are few. There are, of course, real difficulties here, it would be foolish not to admit that,

27

but there are also real opportunities. We all have responsibilities, especially those who have the advantage of both languages, and I am fully conscious of my own, so let me end with one or two practical suggestions.

The University of Wales is already in the lead with the publication by its Press of Gerald Morgan's schools anthology of Anglo-Welsh verse next year. If the other publishers in Wales followed that example with more books of Anglo-Welsh interest, as *Llyfrau'r Dryw* intend, including translations from the Welsh and interpretative essays about the Welsh tradition, our schools and colleges in the English-speaking areas would be able to offer a full syllabus of Anglo-Welsh literature which, in my experience, is much more likely to interest children than the grey selections from English Victorian authors that are presented in the schools of Wales. Gerald Morgan has already done pioneer work here, of course. Indeed, since the publication by Aberystwyth's Faculty of Education of his booklet about the teaching of English in the schools of Wales and his appointment to the headmastership of an Anglesey comprehensive school, he is to be regarded as a principal participant in the dialogue. I have every confidence, too, in his talent and ambition as an editor of *Poetry Wales*. But it is high time that the efforts of enthusiastic amateurs of Anglo-Welsh literature were recognised, co-ordinated and supplemented by cultural organisations in Wales. Is it too much to hope, for example, that when the Academy of Welsh Writers is able to expand and open its doors to painters and musicians, as was its original intention, it may also provide a place, perhaps an autonomous section based on the Guild of (Anglo-)Welsh writers, for the Anglo-Welsh? Already, such writers as R.S. Thomas, Glyn Jones, Emyr Humphreys, all Welsh speakers but whose creative work is done in English, have been invited to become members. If the Academy decided that its role was to foster and represent all the writers of Wales, whether Welsh or Anglo-Welsh, I am sure it would become not only a powerful patron within our borders but an influential spokesman for the literature of Wales to the world, like the P.E.N. in other countries. With such a splendid role in mind, I suggest that the Academy should sponsor a conference, bilingual and using the instantaneous translation systems now available, at which Welsh and Anglo-Welsh writers could meet to discuss their problems, discover common ground and enquire whether a fruitful association might be planned for the future.

I have singled out the Academy because I see no point in trying to make room for the Anglo-Welsh on the stage of the National Eisteddfod. As I hope was made quite clear by the open letter that a majority of Anglo-Welsh writers sent to the Eisteddfod council last October, we have no interest in literary competitions in the English language. Our sympathy with the Welsh language and its literature demands that the Welsh rule must be firmly kept. But I, for one, would like to see some recognition made to Anglo-Welsh writers, perhaps an award like the Gold Medal that goes every year to an artist, never mind what language he speaks. Around such an honour we might then see a vigorous fringe of Anglo-Welsh activities gather, and preferably as an offical part of the Eisteddfod programme, but in the same town and during the same week. At Barry next year, for example, a hall might be hired for poetry readings, exhibitions, plays, discussions and as a social centre for the Welshmen who turn up every year but are unable to participate in the festivities of the *Maes*.

I have made a few proposals towards the opening of 'the dialogue' between Welsh and Anglo-Welsh writers but I must leave the matter there, for the time being, because I do not want to anticipate the exciting projects now under consideration by the Welsh Arts Council for literature in Wales from next year on. I would like to end these notes with an appeal for tolerance, imagination and good will on the part of all who are interested in the bilingual problems of Wales. This is a critical moment in our country's history when one guffaw, one snub, could do irreparable harm. Let the writers set an example to the nation and stop quarrelling for crumbs. Our country's heritage is spread before us and we are all bidden to the feast.

SALLY ROBERTS JONES

Family Ghost

In bed I suddenly wonder why the door is closed;
What else but the known absurdities lie hid
There with the Sunday piano and china nymphs.

Nothing, of course. Open the varnished door,
There's only the Sabbath propriety to see,
Unravished for sixty years; a hymn's last note

Still quavering slightly the butterfly's cane wings.
And yet, it is closed. Hearing a sound in the night,
A foot on the stair, the hint of a breath in the gloom,

Conventional scares: and yet in conventional rooms
More chilling for that. Some bulk of a ghost in the dark
Tightens the throat, presses the air to ice.

Laying this sort of vampire, drive your stake
Hard into brass and snap-shot; open doors —
He you did not see die, will not be laid.

LESLIE NORRIS

Water

On hot summer mornings my aunt set glasses
On a low wall outside the farmhouse,
With some jugs of cold water.
I would sit in the cold hall, or
   Behind the dairy window,
Waiting for the children to come from the town.

They came in small groups, serious, steady,
And I could see them, black in the heat,
Long before they turned in at our gate
To march up the soft, dirt road.
   They would stand by the wall,
Drinking water with an engrossed thirst. The dog

Did not bother them, knowing them responsible
Travellers. They held in quiet hands their bags
Of jam sandwiches, and bottles of yellow fizz.
Sometimes they waved a gratitude to the house,
   But they never looked at us.
Their eyes were full of the mountain, lifting

Their measuring faces above our long hedge.
When they had gone I would climb the wall,
Looking for them among the thin sheep runs.
Their heads were a resolute darkness among ferns,
   They climbed with unsteady certainty.
I wondered what it was they knew the mountain had.

They would pass the last house, Lambert's, where
A violent gander, too old by many a Christmas,
Blared evil warning from his bitten moor,
Then it was open world, too high and clear
   For clouds even, where over heather
The free hare cleanly ran, and the summer sheep.

I knew this; and I knew all summer long
Those visionary gangs passed through our lanes,
Coming down at evening, their arms full
Of cowslips, moondaisies, whinberries, nuts,
   All fruits of the sliding seasons,
And the enormous experience of the mountain

That I who loved it did not understand.
In the summer, dust filled our winter ruts
With a level softness, and children walked

At evening through golden curtains scuffed
　From the road by their trailing feet.
They would drink tiredly at our wall, talking

Softly, leaning, their sleepy faces warm for home.
We would see them murmur slowly through our stiff
Gate, their shy heads gilded by the last sun.
One by one we would gather up the used jugs,
　The glasses. We would pour away
A little water. It would lie on the thick dust, gleaming.

JOHN POOK

Oxbridge Don

Your supervision essay. Yes, it's hard to say.
How about 'The Continuity of English prose?'
Yes, let it be that. It's a subject that grows
On one, I feel, with time and practice —
Only of course with time and practice.
But if you put in a lot of time on it
There is no reason why you should not
Produce a good piece of work.
As for critics on the topic, now let me see,
Ah yes, my wife and I, we
(Ha Ha one should be modest)
Have collaborated on an edition of the works of Rolle.
You know, the English mystic, Richard Rolle?
Oh I see, you don't. Um, oh, er, N.A.B. Macdonald
Has written a good article in 'Medium Aevum' for 1933
You'll find it in the University Library.
Then there's Tatlock of course. Proceedings of the
American Philological Society: Illinois University.
He was visiting professor when I was up at the Varsity.
Very good too, old Freddy. Had some odd ideas though.
He believed (I was remarking on this only today to my wife)
That the study of literature was directly related to life.
Strange really.

NORMAN SCHWENK

To Yeats, Too Late

(Never give all the heart)

Give all the heart. Give it all.
Don't *shove* it at her in a squall
Of blood and tears, though, and then expect
Her thankfully to grab up your delect-
Able organs, one by one, at *your* bloody beck
And call. No, no. You've got to watch and wait.
Give her a chance to see you might be great,
That if she doesn't want your love, O.K.
This isn't a game; it's dead serious play.
So hide your pump behind your back and pray.
And try to stop *shaking*. Let her have a peek
If she seems curious about the leak
Drip dripping dripping — your red penny drops.
But no overtures. Patience. Till she stops
On some baroque off day and says, "Hey, Jack,
I want that funny thing behind your back."
Then give it up. Don't pare off a piece
And ask her if she likes the smell, the taste.
Just give it all. Garnish it on a platter —
Take a deep, gurgly breath, and hand it over.

R.S. THOMAS

Loyalties

The prince walks upon the carpet
Our hearts have unrolled
For him; a worn carpet,
I fear. We are poor
People; we should have saved up

For this; these rents, these blood stains,
This erosion of the edges
Of it, do him no honour.

And where does it lead to
Anyway? Behind the counters
The shopkeepers are all attention.
I would have run it to the door
Of the holding where Puw lived
Once, wrapping the language
About him, watching the trickle
Of his children down the hill's side.

ALAN PERRY

Proverbs And Sayings From The Roadside

It's a long, long trench
that has no turning

Never take five
when you can take six

It takes two
to lift a shovel

Too many foremen
spoil the job

A foreman's work
is never done

Look up
before you light up

Holes have ears

34

It's an ill pick
that strikes a cable

Rolling stones
knock you silly

Drills should be seen
and not heard

Watch your toes
and your feet will look after themselves

Count your wages
before you get them

A pint in the Bird in Hand
is worth two in the Bush

Muck is cleaner
on the other side

People who live in mansions
should be stoned

Navvys might fly

As you dig your hole
so you must lie in it.

GWYN THOMAS

David Gwenallt Jones (1899–1968)

Gwenallt was a small man with a walk that seemed like the quick, delicate and smooth turning of little wheels. Yet the small body generated, like some huge dynamo, so great a sense of energy that one could almost hear it crackle. He had gentle eyes.

But in real gentleness there is also a toughness: Gwenallt was unyielding and uncompromising about what he believed, and he could do and say things that did not please people of conventional attitudes. Indeed it seemed that he sometimes went out of his way to shock.

If one has lived in this country during this century and cares for Wales and the Welsh language it is often difficult not to give way to bitterness. If one is a Christian in the twentieth century it is often easy to yield to a profound pessimism. Gwenallt was a Christian and a nationalist. There is bitterness in his work (see, for example, his poem 'Rhydcymerau' in *Eples*), a bitterness that fuels his wrath against the wrongs he saw in the world. This bitterness and his active credo ensured that he did not give way to despondency. Christian charity, a genuine love of people, compassion for their suffering, and a fighting spirit saved him from the Slough of Despond. No one who achieved the hard serenity of 'Y Meirwon' ('The Dead': see Anthony Conran:*Welsh Verse*, p. 280) or the austere if prose-like dignity of 'Trychineb Aber-fan' ('The Tragedy of Aber-fan', *Taliesin* Vol. 15) could possibly be called despondent. The words of this last poem are like great wounds, the agony of the people of Aber-fan is shown to be connected with the suffering of people in other tragedies and with the agony of Christ. We shall have to rely on translations of the poet's words.

> The sludge of Tip Seven made Aber-fan like Bethlem or
>   Ramah;
> Ramah, where Rahel wept for her children because they were not
> And would not be comforted: the enemy moved the children
> In bondship into Babylon, but in bondship at least there is life,
> And where there is life there is hope. Herod cut off with the
>   sword
> The heads of children in Bethlem, but though the children were
>   corpses their mothers
> Knew them. If there is killing, better be killed with a blade than
>   with mud.
> The mothers of Aber-fan weep heart-broken, especially the
>   mothers of children
> Who could not be known; they weep the most bitter tears of the
>   twentieth century; tears

That were deeper than the tears of mothers in Bethlem, and
  deeper than the tears of Rahel.
Some mothers stand like images before the glutinous deluge
  believing
That it was all a nightmare, a nightmare that came to them the
  night before.
Some are jealous of the living children; others bitter with God
That He did not fall from heaven to stop the tip from vomiting
  its death:
Some search for the murderer of their children to hang him high
  on the Hanging Tree.
Parents feel the eternal arms closing about them, holding them
  up,
Holding their wounded faith in Christ, and their shattered hope
  in God.
No member can ever worship Him again in Bethania
Because the corpses of their children have lain there, left
  without farewell,
Without one cry, without fondle . . . .

In suffering there is a deep, a deep that pulls
Men, women and children together, near to one another.

Christ also descended into this deep — "He lost the Father, in
the three-hour dark after the eclipse"; but His suffering was
"deeper than the suffering of Aber-fan". The Cross is a sign of
forgiveness and love, a "knot that catastrophe cannot break".
The poem ends with the following lines:

In that piece of land above is the great Cross of flowers, and on
  it
The wreath from San Remo: and on the graves are the little
  crosses, small and neighbourly;
On every grave, except the grave of the unknown dead, there is
  a name.
The Cross of our faith and our salvation. The Cross of
  righteousness and love.

Once, the man who made this Christian poem had inwardly
cursed the sermon and the God of the preacher who had said in
the funeral service for his father that the death was 'the will of
God'. Gwenallt's father was burnt to death in the steel works;

37

molten metal fell upon him. When Gwenallt went away from home and was given his membership paper by his home chapel he threw it into the fire.

What I propose to do for the remainder of this article is to provide a commentary on Gwenallt's own article in the book *Credaf* (ed. J.E. Meredith, Gwasg Aberystwyth, 1943) and to back this commentary with references to his work. It will be a commentary on how Gwenallt rediscovered his Christian faith.

Unlike many Welsh poets Gwenallt was born in an industrial town, Pontardawe in Glamorganshire. His parents came from Carmarthenshire and, as a boy, he used to visit his family in the country. His father was a poet who had won chairs in local eisteddfodau. He bought for his son Dafydd Morgannwg's *Ysgol Farddol*, a manual on traditional Welsh metres and *cynghanedd*. As a result of this, and the interest shown at home, Gwenallt came to know these things and to practise them at an early age.

The family, like many other families in Wales at the beginning of this century, were great chapel-goers. On a typical Sunday Gwenallt would have gone to the morning service, to Sunday-school in the afternoon, to a 'Five-Meeting' where the young were taught to pray in public, to the evening service, and then to the *Ysgol Gân* (singing practice). And during the week (on 'working nights') he would have attended the *Seiat* and the Prayer Meeting.

As a boy he used to take his father's 'dinner' to him in the steel works.

> There I saw [the furnace] being 'tapped' and the molten metal flowing into the ladle in the pit, and from the ladle to the moulds, and after it had set the crane lifted it in steel sheets and placed them in stacks by the tramway. I used to be afraid when I saw the tallon of the crane swinging the ingot above the men in the pit.

In 1910 there was a strike in the steel works. With other boys Gwenallt enjoyed scraping for coal in disused mine-shafts or on tips, enjoyed seeing policemen escorting 'blacklegs' to and from the works. He used to say that he and some of his friends once placed stones on the edge of a railway cutting where they knew some policmen had to pass below. When they did pass the boys pushed the stones on top of them and ran away.

But the bitterness that was part of these pranks surfaced as Gwenallt became more and more aware of the hardship of the workers. He began to ask why things should be as they were; what sort of Christianity did they have in the chapels if they were willing to endure poverty and hardship. These were also the kinds of questions that were being asked by Socialists, and were the questions of many of the Independent Labour Party. Gwenallt aligned himself with them. What was needed was an economic revolution, the destruction of capitalism, the system through which Gwenallt thought a few grew fat whilst the majority starved.

From this harsh judgement of the Christianity of the chapels he went on to criticize Christianity itself, and gradually he came under the influence of Communism. When the Great War came in 1914, Gwenallt saw it as a war to defend an unjust capitalist economy and he refused to participate in any way. Like some other conscientious objectors he was imprisoned and spent some time in Wormwood Scrubs and Dartmoor. His novel, ironically entitled *Plasau'r Brenin* (The King's Mansions) is based on his experiences in prison, as is the poem 'Dartmoor' (see Conran, p. 80).

In 1919 he went to the University College of Wales, Aberystwyth. There he was introduced to the work of the English Romantic poets and the work of aesthetes like Arthur Symons, Ernest Dowson and Walter Pater. He also became acquainted with the work of several French poets of the nineteenth and twentieth centuries. He began to think that passion was the most important thing in life and literature, a swooning after the beautiful and a love of art for its own sake. This period can best be explained as a rather superficial reaction to the hard materialism of much that had gone before. Its influence, though in a more mature way, is to be seen to some extent on Gwenallt's '*Awdlau-Y Mynach*' (The Monk), '*Y Sant*' (The Saint) and '*Breuddwyd y Bardd*' (The Poet's Dream).

But what had gone before could not be forgotten. In the poet's subconscious were his readings of Tolstoi, Dostoievsky, Marx, Lenin; the poverty and the strikes in South Wales, "and in my nostrils [was] the memory of the unnatural smell of coffins in the parlours of the workers."

In 1924 a Labour government was elected. Whilst he acknowledged that it did some good, Gwenallt was disappointed:

> The King remained on his throne, the House of Lords was not abolished; instead Labour peers went into the House. Labour 'peers' for crying out loud!

These words show that he was, in fact, searching for an ideal. His disappointment with the short-lived Labour government of 1924 led him to a closer examination of Communism too, and to another disappointment. He began to realize that human systems as such are bound to fall short of expectations. He felt that the reason for this was man's selfishness.

The search for some kind of salvation now turns to the individual rather than to systems; it now becomes self-examination. And just as Baudelaire found in his kind of society that material change had very little to do with what was really important to a human being and came face to face with the flaw in human personality that theologians call Original Sin, so Gwenallt also felt his way in his society to a similar conclusion about man.

Gwenallt accepted Christianity as the way of true life. This was a pervasive and comprehensive Christianity and not one that went in its Sunday best.

> The span of the Cross is far greater
> Than their Puritanism and their Socialism,
> And there's a place for the fist of Karl Marx in His Church:
> Farm and furnace go together in His estate,
> The humanity of the pit, the piousness of the country:
> Tawe and Tywi, Canaan and Wales, earth and heaven.

After graduating, Gwenallt was a school-teacher for a brief period until he was appointed lecturer in the Department of Welsh in his old college at Aberystwyth. He remained in the department until his retirement in 1966. For some time after his appointment he regarded his literary studies as more of an exercise in antiquarianism than anything else. He thought there was far too much boring Christianity and boring nationalism in the literature of his country's past. For anyone who is familiar with his poetry this may be surprising. It was whilst he was attending a summer school in Spideal, Ireland, in 1929 that he fully realized the value of a country's language and its indigenous culture, and the importance of the past in its bearing on the present. He now saw beyond his own industrial upbringing, he saw the connection between his own life and the life that had gone on for generations and centuries in Carmarthenshire where his family had its roots. For him this was an establishing of an identity within a tradition and the realization of a pattern that spanned centuries. His nationalism, like his socialism, finds a place within the Christian experience in his work. This was how he sang to the muse in his volume of poetry, *Gwreiddiau* (Roots).

> But today the Muse is the breath that God has given the artist.
> Like that ingenious breath that Bezaleel son of Uri received long
>   ago:
> And the Christian Muse of the poets of Wales from Cynddelw
>   Brydydd
> To Elfed was the gift of the light and the wind;
> And to make this first gift to shine is our privilege and our task;
> The Muse of Christmas and Good Friday, the Pentecost and
>   Easter.

What Gwenallt achieved was a cohesion of various experiences within his Christian vision of life.

Gwenallt died on Christmas Eve, 1968. But he saw beyond his own death:

Cyn hir fe fydd fy nghorpws	Before long this little body
Yn gig i bryfed brwd,	Will be flesh for fervent worms,
A phlât yr arch a'i thrimins	The coffin lid, bright trimmings
Disglair yn fyw gan rwd.	Will be eaten up by rust.
Bydd haul uwch dyffryn Tywi	The sun will be above the Tywi
Fel darn cyfalaf Duw	Like a piece of God's great wealth
Ni all y pryf ei gyrraedd,	The worm can never reach it
Ni lyga'r rhwd ei liw.	Nor rust its colour corrupt.
(*Cnoi Cil*, p.17)	

JOHN ORMOND

My Grandfather And His Apple Tree

Life sometimes held such sweetness for him
As to engender guilt. From the night vein he'd come,
From working in water wrestling the coal,
Up the pit slant. Every morning hit him
Like a journey of trams between the eyes;
A wild and drinking farmboy sobered by love
Of a miller's daughter and a whitewashed cottage
Suddenly to pay rent for. So he'd left the farm
For dark under the fields six days a week
With mandrel and shovel and different stalls.
All light was beckoning. Soon his hands
Untangled a brown garden into neat greens.

There was an apple tree he limed, made sturdy;
The fruit was sweet and crisp upon the tongue
Until it budded temptation in his mouth.
Now he had given up whistling on Sundays,
Attended prayer-meetings, added a concordance
To his wedding Bible and ten children
To the village population. He nudged the line,
Clean-pinafored and collared, glazed with soap,
Every seventh day of rest in Ebenezer;
Shaved on a Saturday night to escape the devil.

The sweetness of the apples worried him.
He took a branch of cooker from a neighbour
When he became a deacon, wanting
The best of both his worlds. Clay from the colliery
He thumbed about the bole one afternoon
Grafting the sour to sweetness, bound up
The bleeding white of junction with broad strips
Of working flannel-shirt and belly-bands
To join the two in union. For a time
After the wound healed the sweetness held,
The balance tilted towards an old delight.

But in the time that I remember him
(His wife had long since died, I never saw her)
The sour half took over. Every single apple
Grew — across twenty Augusts — bitter as wormwood.
He'd sit under the box-tree, his pink gums
(Between the white moustache and goatee beard)
Grinding thin slices that his jack-knife cut,
Sucking for sweetness vainly. It had gone,
Gone. I heard him mutter
Quiet Welsh oaths as he spat the gall-juice
Into the seeding onion-bed, watched him toss
The big core into the spreading nettles.

ROLFE HUMPHRIES

For My Ancestors

Cyhydded fer

Wales, which I have never seen,
Is gloomy, mountainous, and green,
And, as I judge from reading Borrow,
The people there rejoice in sorrow,
Dissenters, most of them, and cranks,
Surly and churlish, grudging thanks,
Suspicious, dour, morose, perplexed,
And just a little oversexed.
Mostly, however, they go in
More for remorsefulness than sin,
The latter being prior to
The real delight, of feeling blue.
Fellows named Morgan, Evans, Jones,
Sit glumly on the ancient stones,
And men with names in — IES,
Like mine, lurk in the wilderness
With conscience riding on their shoulders
Heavier than the native boulders.

The weather veers from dim to foul,
The letter W's a vowel;
They dig in mines, they care for sheep,
Some kinds of promises they keep;
They can remember warriors found
Dead in green armour on green ground;
They practice magic out of season,
They hate the English with good reason,
Nor do they trust the Irish more,
And find the Scots an utter bore.
However grim their life, and hard,
One thing they dearly love, a bard.
Even the meanest hand at lays
Is plied with ale, and crowned with bays,
And set with honour in their books
Above even liars, thieves, and crooks.
This is the one redeeming grace
That saves them for the human race,
This is their claim to virtue; therefore,
Though there is much I do not care for
In my inheritance, I own
This impulse in my blood and bone,
And so I bend a reverent knee,
O Cymric ancestor, to thee, —
Wild Wales forever! Foul or fair,
This tribute from a grateful heir.

JOSEPH CLANCY

Confession

Never in fifteen years of
Marriage could I manage to
Say *I love you* and know I
Meant it as much, dear, as you,
A full submerging of self,

44

And even at the peak of
Our tenderest conjunction
You gave yourself to the full,
Surpassed me in surrender,
Something within me shut tight
As the seedy gift spurted,
Refusing to lose myself.

I thank God for these last four
Years of fearing my dying,
For the stabs in arms and chest,
The dizziness, the nausea,
The struggle to survive each
Day's journeying to the job,
The hours spent in the classroom
Sick, sweating, striving to hide
Behind my booming reading
Of verse my fear of collapse.
My death was a fact I took
For the first time as something
Real, that might lunge from ambush
Any moment in the day.
No surprise in my horror
Of annihilation, despite
Belief in a hereafter,
But wonder to find my mind
Ridden by dread, if I died,
For you and for the children,
Counting the years I somehow
Must go on till they were grown
To aid and not to burden
Your bare self-dependent days.

Was this love, alive at last,
Begotten by this terror,
Or had it, for all those years,
Beat the bars, or lain dormant?
No matter: I celebrate
That selflessness, what little

I learned, having earned the right
To say at last *I love you*,
Though never in your fashion,
Meaning part of what it means.

HARRI WEBB

Cywydd

*of praise and thanks
to the Welsh Arts Council*

Flap we our lips, praise Big Man,
Bards, religious Shire Cardigan —
Not frogs croaking are we
Nor vain crows but bards tidy;
Wise is our speak, like Shadrach.
Hearken you now, people bach,
Mouth some: Cardiff ach y fi,
Not holy like Aberteifi!

Twp it is to speech so,
In Cardiff is gold yellow.
White Jesus bach, let no ill
Befall Big Heads Arts Council.
Pounds they have, many thousand,
Like full till shop draper grand,
Truth it is and no fable,
All for bards respectable.
Good is the work they are at,
Soaped they shall be in Seiat,
Reserved shall be for them
A place in Big Seat Salem.
Praised let them be for this thing,
Money they are distributing
Like Beibil moses his manna.
Tongue we all, bards Welsh, Ta.

46

RAYMOND GARLICK

Explanatory Note

For some of us, you see,
Wales is another word for peace.
The changing of the guard
Is not our national frontispiece.
We like our castles ruined.
Mountains green as the verdigris

Overlaying old armour
Are our image — in millpond lakes.
Wales is a word for life
Without kings and lords, and the cakes
Of living expertly sliced
Into great wedges, slender flakes.

Wales is two languages,
Not one: and both of them invoke
A ritual dragon
Trampling a meadow green as oak
In one half; but the other —
White as Gandhi's cloak.

GILLIAN CLARKE

Lines

Diagonally the line
Dips between the tree
And the house. It wavers
Like the uncertain edge of a flag,
At the same time dividing
The space, charting one triangle

With clean white gestures,
And pegging together with small,
Desperate wooden teeth
The closed wound.

Ostensibly I lie
Sunbathing. I can feel
That wound of the divided
Mind: the upper triangle
Is rational. The aspens
Spinning leaves like florins
Up there in the light
Assert that it was good
For me, the pain.

    Below
In the other part, the blind,
Blue, polythene pool,
Trawling coins and the dark
Sides of aspen moons,
Holds but sees no light.
The laundered people drown
In my pool. They wave
Their fistless arms, irregular
As images in a hall
Of mirrors.

    At the end
Of the day I stood up, shook
The mysterious black prism
Watching the circles and flakes
Of light falling, and a red,
Plastic steamer, going
Nowhere, bumping the sides
Like a moth at a shut
Window. The shapes fell
In a coloured muddle on the grass.
Neatly, slowly I folded
Clothes, and survived.

JOHN STUART WILLIAMS

In Marienbad

They move through the night
as softly as a rose unfolds.
In Marienbad the stairways soar
like hyacinths, the tight

clocks have no hands
and a single magpie
plunders the wild strawberries.
Time sifts the hour-glass sands.

Look, the yellow grains
flow upwards, the glass
itself dissolves and the sea,
implacable as logic, complains

in the leaves of this inland birch.
Who drives through the darkness
with such intensity?
Who knows how the day will march?

JEREMY HOOKER

The Poetry Of David Jones

In his book *Language and Silence*, George Steiner wrote,
"among prolegomena to future forms, one would also want to
include . . . the work of David Jones." Dr. Steiner does not
elaborate the remark, but it is clear from context that what he has
in mind is largely the deliberate breakdown effected by David
Jones of hard and fast rules governing the distinction between
poetry and prose. Now this is a breakdown which, I believe,
assimilates the prose to the intensity of the poetry while retaining

the prose's faculty of elucidation, so that the whole — *The Anathemata,* for example — does not give the switchback sensation of descending abruptly from moments of intensity into hollows of prosaic commentary but does afford remarkable variations of tone, rhythm, and pitch. It also makes possible an enormous range of reference, dramatic and narrative complexity, and the beauty of visual designs on the page, while illustrating Eliot's idea that a poet who attempts long poems must be capable of writing good prose. For David Jones is a master of prose, as those who have had the pleasure of reading *Epoch and Artist* will agree. He has developed a highly wrought style, itself akin to poetry, more in the mode of Joyce than of any other modern writer, but owing something to the mannered dignity of Malory. The style alone shows how much of the past David Jones has, in absorbing it, made his own; and for that very reason both style and form introduce us to the apparent paradox fundamental to his work. David Jones, a writer who has consciously developed his own individual style of the modernism we associate principally with Eliot, Joyce, and Pound, has, like them, sought to open connections with the remote past.

Clearly the form of *In Parenthesis* and *The Anathemata* has affinities with the "prose interspersed with speech poems" used by the ancient poets and "known in ancient Egypt as in medieval Europe, in Vedic India as in modern Ireland," (see Alwyn D. Rees and Brinley Rees: *Celtic Heritage,* p.16). In consequence, the subject-matter, like the form, by the very life in which it is renewed in the poems, belies any attempt to assign it to the "remote past." What is remote? What is past? It is questions such as these that the poems challenge us to answer.

For any one now writing about David Jones the challenge does not end there. After all, the tide of most modern criticism is running against both the manner and the method of his writing, and even in Wales, where he has many admirers, one feels that his position as one of the greatest Anglo-Welsh writers, as well as the one to give the title Anglo-Welsh its most profound significance, is not always recognised. So, with the aim of meeting this challenge in a small way, I want to concentrate here on drawing out the meaning Anglo-Welsh has in relation to his writings.

Being of Welsh and English descent, David Jones might be said, were it that easy, to have the best of both worlds. But the matter is more difficult. As he himself is at all times quick to point out, English is the only language he knows. And yet it is another paradox of this remarkable writer that no other modern poet in English has given such prominence in his work to Wales and the Welsh language. As far as one of his monoglot fellows can judge, the dignity, the power, and the presiding genius of that language are presented, without sentimentality, in the way in which he uses it, especially in *The Anathemata, The Hunt,* and *The Sleeping Lord.* It is as if, without speaking Welsh, he can convey a strong impression of its spirit and meaning to an English reader. In fact, one can eschew generalities: David Jones knows, with the insight of a Welshman and the detachment of a Londoner, the part Welsh has played in shaping the cultural complex of which he writes; and, in consequence, he is able to educate both English and Welsh in the things individual to each, and common to both. Of the Celtic cycle, he wrote, in *In Parenthesis,* that it "lies, a subterranean influence as a deep water troubling, under every tump in this Island, like Merlin complaining under his big rock." Wales is a similar influence in David Jones's poetry.

"This Island" may seem, to people with diverse viewpoints, an old-fashioned, even a distasteful, way of speaking about Britain; it may be redolent to them of all manner of unpleasant rhetoric, sentimentality, or political eyewash. It often is used in those ways. David Jones is the only modern writer I know who can use the expression meaningfully without evoking a shadow of imperialist cant. And this is because Britain, as a complex of diverse entities, not as a word used for England just because it sounds bigger, is his subject-matter. Thus, to make this subject-matter live, he has to combat all forms of abstraction, expecially those by means of which England and Wales are reduced to antagonistic formulae. In pursuit of this aim he achieves, like Hopkins, whom he so much admires, a poetry committed to the sensuous embodiment of particular things. As with the Jesuit, his metaphysic demands it.

His material, then, is the different cultures by which he, a Londoner closely connected to England and Wales, has been shaped, and which he sees as fundamental to the making of

Britain. The elements he conceives to be especially important in that making — the Celtic foundations of Pre-Roman Britain, the unifying power of Rome, the Teutonic warrior-bands — he sees in the light of Christianity. And he is concerned above all with what now exists, a complex of diverse elements which have undergone the political tendency of recent centuries to reduce them to a single unit unconscious of its true nature, a narrow Englishness unaware of what its roots are. Thus what *The Anathemata* commemorates is no less than the physical making of Britain's landform and the growth upon it of these roots. David Jones brings the English reader to a Wales that is in no sense England with a foreign tongue but is, nevertheless, far less alien to him than he realizes. The poem is an heroic attempt to place the inheritors of Angle-land in the richer culture that the Celtic peoples have retained.

This concern with Britain as a unity comprising different peoples is evident in *In Parenthesis*. There, the Welsh and Cockney soldiers, drawn together by force of war, re-enact the creation of a common heritage. The poet, who is part of the experience, sees the past come alive in them in a way which, despite their diverse backgrounds, evokes other events that have brought them together — the Crimea, the wars of Henry V — and also something fundamental to all of them, the mythological 'deposits' of the Island. Soldiers of an Empire which still comprehends living differences, they bring different traditions to the common folly imposed upon them, and out of it make a real unity — as opposed to the military unit — in the folk-life to which each contributes. And from the disturbance and upheaval there emerges, for the poet, the powerful contemporary significance of Celtic mythology so that the trenches evoke "the frozen regions of the Celtic underworld":

> Do dogs of Annwn glast this starving air — do they ride the trajectory zone, between the tangled brake above the leaning walls.
> This seventh gate is parked tonight.
> His lamps hang in this black cold and hang so still; with this still rain slow-moving vapours wreathe to refract their clear ray — like through glassy walls that slowly turn they rise and fracture — for this fog-smoke wraith they cast a dismal sheen.

It is not only that the poet's imagination is alive to these chilling legends and therefore open to the charge — insultingly made by D.J. Enright in *The Modern Age* — of imposing a literary image upon an experience alien to it; the new horrors show the permanent experiential validity of these legends by recalling them. Again, "the persistent Celtic theme of armed sleepers under the mounds" is called up for David Jones by "the tumbled undulations and recesses, the static sentries, and the leaning arms that were the Forward Zone." Arthur, principal of these sleepers, is never far from the poet's mind.

In *In Parenthesis* he sees Arthur as "the Protector of the Land, the Leader, the Saviour, the Lord of Order carrying a raid into the place of Chaos." Later, in *The Sleeping Lord*, Arthur becomes identified with Wales. It is at this point of my argument that, acknowledging the damage a crude prose exposition can do to the delicate web of his metaphysic, something must be said about the place in all this of Christianity.

For David Jones the Celtic foundations are all of a piece with Christianity. For him the pagan past with its worship and sacrifice was the foreshadowing of the Christian order, so that Christ and the Virgin Mary fulfil all those needs expressed by the human spirit in primitive religion. Christianity, one could say, is the one unifying force that David Jones, the poet who celebrates the unique individual differences born of the marriage between people and place, finds creative; and for him it is the principle of creativity. To each place its own genius, a genius deriving from the female creative principle which the Catholic poet finds embodied in its highest form in the Mother of God. Christ is the Lord of Order, but what He orders is personality, unique individual things which uniformity — military, technological, or imperial — tries to destroy. For David Jones the personality of Britain, that which because it is creative embodies the true nature of man, is intimately bound up with the fate of Wales. It is there, in the genius of place, that he sees the foundations preserved, which an increasing tendency towards uniformity obliterates. Hence, in the poems, use of the Welsh language, whereby the pattern of sound is consonant with English and Latin words, serves as a verbal and historical recalling of the other element in the making of Britain which England mostly forgets about. In this example, from *The Sleeping Lord,* he is speaking of Christ:

> of the shepherd of Greekland
>   the Heofon-Cyning
> born of Y Forwyn Fair
>   lapped in hay in the ox's stall
> next the grey ass in the caved *stabulum*
> *ad praesepem* in heye Bedlem
>   that is bothe bryht and schen.

In 'Mabinog's Liturgy' (*The Anathemata*), the birth of Christ is retold in the form of a marvel-tale of birth in the Welsh tradition. The use of Welsh enacts the process by which Christianity, the universal order, is made native to each separate place, not, as with an Empire, by reducing the language of that place to its own alien tongue, but, by marriage to the genius of place, preserving its individual identity. (As in Irish tradition the King was sometimes said to marry the land.) More impressive than the example given above is the passage in 'Rite and Fore-Time' (*The Anathemata*) describing the physical making of Wales:

> Before the slow estuarine alchemies had coal-blacked the green dryad-ways over the fire-clayed seat-earth along all the utile seams from Taff to Táf.
>
> Before the microgranites and the clay-bonded erratics wrenched from the diorites of Aldasa, or off the Goat Height in the firth-way, or from the Clota-sides or torn from either Dalriada, with what was harrowed-out *in via*, up, from the long drowned out-crops, under, coalesced and southed by the North Channel.
>   As though the sea itself were sea-borne
>   and under weigh
>   as if the whole Iverniam *mare*
> directed from hyperboreal control-points by strategi of the axis were one complex of formations in depth, moving on a frontage widening with each lesser degree of latitude.
>   Heading toward, right astride
> to one degree beyond
>   Ffraid Santes' fire-track
> where Brendan shall cry from his sea-horse
> *Mirabilis Deus in sanctis suis!*

A plethora of anachronisms, of course, to any one incapable of understanding the Christian vision shaping the passage, by which, even in its geological making, the genius of place already participates in the Christian order.

The later Arthurian poems, *The Hunt* and *The Sleeping Lord*, in which Arthur is presented as a type of Christ, have an intensity that can only be described as devotional. It is as if, disturbed by the general blankness which greeted the vision of Britain expressed in *The Anathemata*, David Jones has turned his energies to showing, while there is still time, how Wales has in keeping the foundational things; as if, too, he is turning away from England to Wales as the only place where what he is writing about will be understood. Other poems, such as *The Tribune's Visitation*, show with frightening clarity the forces intent on destroying those things in the name of a false order. True, he is writing that poem about Rome, but the analogy is clear to see. The past is not remote. On the one hand, what Rome as an Empire stood for in its totalitarian phase is present at any time when the creative life of a place is shown convincing reasons for its rationalization; on the other, where that life refuses to succumb it is ultimately in the name of a higher order than uniformity.

It can be seen that David Jones's poetry in breaking new ground formally derives some of its originality from the connections he has made with ancient and modern methods and materials. (If *The Anathemata* makes one think, at times, of Joyce, Eliot, or Hopkins, it also contains a *Polyolbion*.) At a time when English poetry is turning ever more rapidly from the stultifying limitations of the ironic pose and the confines of such fiftyish attitudes as that rejecting the use of myth and all but immediate, rather middle-class experience as the occasion for poetry, there is a good chance that David Jones will be widely rediscovered as one offering an alternative to the dying fashions. Even for poets who do not share his religion, he can offer, to my mind, at least as much as Pound's *Cantos* and recent American poetry in the field of rhythm, movement, and overall shape — a matter poets will appreciate who have struggled against the iambic confinement of traditional form. Moreover, discovering David Jones, even for those unmoved by what they find, leads on to other discoveries, to a wealth of native poetry in English and

Welsh which reveals what can be done to extend the imagination far beyond the limits of domestic experience; it leads to history, which is where Anglo-Welsh poetry has always been: discovering in place the foundations of human community.

For other poets David Jones has opened up sources of myth and history, and a world of ideas remarkable in the specific detail as in the overall design. If I have understood the principal aims of Anglo-Welsh poetry correctly as the search for roots, the commemoration of a past still sufficiently present to give life, and the criticism of the tendencies alien to that life's survival, then David Jones is the most important poet pursuing these aims, and his work shows that they are, in fact, related to a single aim. Finally, I cannot think of a better definition of Anglo-Welsh poetry than as one which is itself the marriage of two languages, in word or in spirit, and of all that each embodies.

MEIC STEPHENS

Hooters

Night after night from my small bed
I heard the hooters blowing up and down the cwm:
Lewis Merthyr, Albion, Nantgarw, Ty-draw —
these were the familiar banshees of my boyhood.

For each shift they hooted, not a night
without the high moan that kept me from sleep;
often, as my father beyond the thin wall
rumbled like the turbines he drove at work, I

stood for hours by the box-room window,
listening. The dogs of Annwn barked for me then,
Trystan called without hope to Esyllt
across the black waters. Ai, it was their wail

I heard that night a Heinkel flew up
the Taff and its last bomb fell on our village;

we huddled under the cwtsh, making
beasts against the candle's light until the sky

was clear once more, and the hooters
sounded. I remember too how their special din
brought ambulances to the pit yard,
the masked men coming up the shaft with corpses

gutted by fire; then, as the big cars
moved down the blinded row on the way to Glyntâf,
all the hooters for twenty miles about
began to swell, a great hymn grieving the heart.

Years ago that was. I had forgotten
the hooters: my disasters, these days, are less
spectacular. We live now in this city:
our house is large, detached and behind fences.

I sleep easily, but waking tonight
found the same desolate clangour in my ears
that from an old and sunken level
used to chill me as a boy — the inevitable hooter

that paralyses with its mute alarm.
How long I have been standing at this window,
a man in the grown dark, only my wife
knows as I make for her white side, shivering.

GWYN WILLIAMS

Skull Of The World: Cadbury Hill

No navel of the universe here,
no feeling of being at the centre
of things, buttoning an inland sea,

but a sense of living on a rim
on the flung edge of a way
of life, of survival, of holding

one's head above a flood.
A cranium of hill crowned
wide with great ringing earthworks.

No Gothic keeps here, no ladies
in steeple hats, no horseshow
jousting, no Sir this or that,

good Celtic names corrupted.
A tough life, enough grass for tactics
on horseback, a base for clean cuts

through the creeping enemy, a hall
columned in wood for living,
loving and celebration, a place

for a leader — *penn* — a head,
a head of the western world,
a head of hill with one people

to the west and another on the plains
and sly valleys to the east.
A skull today of a decayed

body, or a rediscovered head
bare in this broken western sky,
to be stockaded in the mind?

JOHN TRIPP

Elegy For Jack Jones

I first heard of you when I was a boy
plundering the library shelves in Eglwys Newydd,
hot for Hemingway with his clean chisel
but seeing your monument to the human cost
of coal and the wound to our valleys.

Even then you were known for your quirks,
the taciturn block of granite
supping his ale and moving his dominoes
in the sawdust tavern. But we marked
your fortitude against the drummer of calamity.

Tenacious scribe, you were never an abstract
philosopher or a literary mechanic who tinkered
with the creative engine. God was in his heaven
and real writers wrote, stubborn in their passage.
You raised your hat in the cemetery of chroniclers.

About four winters back you cuffed the elbow
of my slight life in the big plush hotels
of this town, lording with Merthyr wit
the business of our eminent club. I see now your fine
Lear head, gnarled blue-scarred hands, worn oatmeal jacket.

Once, coming down the darkened bogsteps of the Queens,
you roared at me who was on his way up:
'It's worse than the bloody pit down here, boy!'
I laughed, and loved your undefeated gusto.
You belonged to that tougher Wales before the wildcats left.

And once I saw you leave the Monico
from your free, respected pensioner's pew,
content to watch the pap on a matinée screen.
Then you'd walk back to your ancient keys
on a table in a room where the narratives began.

I remember that sad last birthday at the inn,
surrounded by friends, and the picture for a loyal press.
We jugged-up in your great oak shadow
and wished you well. Outside, the wind's brute bite
started to cut into your falling year.

I remember, too, when Glyn and I
on a steel day sat by your hearth in silence,
the fire dead-banked inside you, and grief in the eyes
for the Leveller you knew would soon stoop
tapping on your door in Rhiwbeina.

But first came the honour your land had given,
the short tingling speech which you turned
with a couple of stories. Here was a moment
we who were there would never forget —
a doyen's dignity hacked from disaster.

Jack, this is only a thin reminiscence,
the few late leaves of a stripling sprinter
fiddling on a scene you dominioned for so long.
But I come of your stock, a flaccid version
longing for a gold-leaf piece of scripture.

Your red unyielded pennant still flutters in requiem.
And today when I visit my kin
bedded in Pantmawr, I look up at the old thunder
in our Welsh sky, and then glance across,
across the lost mounds to your quiet grave.

R.S. THOMAS

Chat

What's that you say?
No never. Well, just once . . . .
Oh, in Paris or somewhere.

She was so pretty. Imagine
Yourself in an hotel
Dining-room; the tables engaged
All save yours. There comes in
A woman, young, soignée;
Looks around, summons the head
Waiter. They confer. He approaches:
Would Monsieur? I arise;
She is seated. Slowly the conversation
Develops. She is well-informed.
I incline; would she allow?
Good. Waiter, some more
Claret. Over the glass
Rim a momentary fencing
Of eyes. Touché, touché:
This is my own blood,
Rich as mahogany,
She is drinking. I present
A new guard: this evening
Mademoiselle no doubt
Is engaged? No! Then . . . ?
She tosses her curls, dandles
A small smile. It
Is not far; we will
Walk. In the spring gardens
All the birds of the city
In song. I begin to speak
As a poet. Like a Beatrice
She listens. The Faubourg
Is left behind; the boulevard
Narrows. There is no
Birdsong now; my rhymes
Falter. But the body
Is all awake, struggling
With no will to escape
From the meshes she has drawn
About me. An alley
Arrests her. I look
At the dark door at the end

That is like the gravestone
Of Villon, of Baudelaire, blistered
With the laughter of the whores
Of Paris . . . What was that
That you said? Well, yes,
I was taken in, I suppose.

SAM ADAMS

The Synge Exhibition

The bird he mounted and his butterflies,
A receipt from Dublin's Naturalists' Club,
The solitary sceptic's violin;

A Paris diary, precise, in French,
Noting, in December, 1896 —
"Fait le connaissance de W.B. Yeates."

His camera, a brown box, beady-eyed;
The careful sepia photographs he took —
The Macdonagh cottage on Inishman,
Aran's shawled women and bonneted men,
Their baskets and nets on Kilronan quay.
Letters from friends in beautiful Gaelic.

His spreadeagled spidery hand at speed,
And an unbelievable typewriter —

"Will you go into the little room
and stretch yourself a short while on the bed.
I'm thinking it's destroyed you are
walking the length of that way in the great rain."

Outside a heavy sky presses the roofs,
Clean rain persists, but with a whiff of Liffey
My drenched coat drips on the library floor.

62

RAYMOND GARLICK

Public Gallery

Your worships (as they say), with all respect
You're not what I had been led to expect.

I sit and observe you over my glasses.
Conduct like this would not do in my classes.

Pert or insolent, mute, uncritical,
No Welsh at all, and English pitiful —

How did you get there? Whose nomination?
What conceivable qualification?

The usual, no doubt. Bourgeois ambition,
Freemasonry, party composition.

You are the British predilection
For amateurism, in local section.

Scarcely surprising that things have gone wrong.
We have been absent from our courts too long

(For they are our courts) — the critical,
The articulate, the professional.

Compare the quality of the defendants
With that of justice's blind attendants.

Appalled, I watch the alienation
Of the finest minds of a generation.

Your law, your courts, your police, will fall to them.
It is yourselves that your words condemn.

Expect the scourging of the Furies
When these become your judges, juries.

But I am wrong. They are compassionate
And understand what brought you to this state.

As they look down upon you from their places
There in the dock, pity moves their faces.

They contemplate, from the elevation
You force them to, the wreckage of a nation.

GLYN JONES

The Common Path

On one side the hedge, on the other the brook.
    Each afternoon I, unnoticed, passed
The middle-aged schoolmistress, grey-haired,
    Gay, loving, who went home along the path.

That spring she walked briskly, carrying her bag
    With the long ledger, the ruler, the catkin twigs,
Two excited little girls from her class
    Chattering around their smiling teacher.

Summer returned, each day then she approached slowly,
    Alone, wholly absorbed, as though in defeat
Between water and hazels, her eyes heedless,
    Her grey face deeply cast down. Could it be
Grief at the great universal agony had begun
    To feed upon her heart — wars, imbecility,
Old age, starving, children's deaths, deformities?
    I, free, white, gentile, born neither
Dwarf nor idiot, passed her by, drawing in
    The skirts of my satisfaction, on the other side.

One day, at the last instant of our passing,
    She became, suddenly, aware of me
And, as her withdrawn glance met my eyes,
    Her whole face kindled into life, I heard

From large brown eyes a blare of terror, anguished
   Supplication, her cry of doom, death, despair.
And in the warmth of that path's sunshine
   And of my small and manageable success
I felt at once repelled, affronted by her suffering,
   The naked shamelessness of that wild despair.

Troubled, I avoided the common until I heard
   Soon, very soon, the schoolmistress, not from
Any agony of remote and universal suffering
   Or unendurable grief for others, but
Private, middle-aged, rectal cancer, was dead.

What I remember, and in twenty years have
   Never expiated, is that my impatience,
That one glance of my intolerance,
   Rejected her, and so rejected all
The sufferings of wars, imprisonments,
   Deformities, starvation, idiocy, old age —
Because fortune, sunlight, meaningless success,
   Comforted an instant what must not be comforted.

LESLIE NORRIS

Bridges

Imagine the bridge launched, its one foot
Clamped hard on bedrock, and such grace
In its growth it resembles flying, is flight
Almost. It is not chance when they speak
Of throwing a bridge; it leaves behind a track
Of its parallel rise and fall, solid
In quarried stone, in timber, in milled
Alloy under stress. A bridge is

The path of flight. A friend, a soldier,
Built a laughable wartime bridge over
Some unknown river. In featureless night
He threw from each slid bank the images
Of his crossing, working in whispers, under
Failing lamps. As they built, braced spars,
Bolted taut the great steel plugs, he hoped
His bridge would stand in brawny daylight, complete,

The two halves airily knit. But
It didn't. They floated above
Midstream, going nowhere, separate
Beginnings of different bridges, offering
Policies of inaction, neither coming
Nor going. His rough men cursed, sloped off,
Forded quite easily a mile lower.
It was shallow enough for his Landrover.

I have a bridge over a stream. Four
Wooden sleepers, simple, direct. After rain,
Very slippery. I rarely cross right over,
Preferring to rest, watching the grain
On running water. I like such bridges best,
River bridges on which men always stand,
In quiet places. Unless I could have that other,
The bridge launched, hovering, wondering where to land.

GLYN JONES

A Letter to the Editor

Dear Meic,

I feel I must offer you my congratulations on your offspring's twenty-first birthday. I spotted the little thing first — this was in 1965, long before I'd met you — in one of the posh bookshops in

Charing Cross Road and I looked at him then, in those rather glamorous surroundings, with some concern. He seemed so frail and puny — only 18 pages! Even the infant *Wales* had 31! Would you, I wondered, as the women of the valleys say in such circumstances, 'rare' him? But now here he is at his majority, fatter and fuller of vitality than ever. You have every reason to feel proud of his survival into such rude health.

Your success makes me think back to the time before anything like *Poetry Wales*, or even *Wales*, existed, to the Twenties and early Thirties, that is. Not being a child prodigy at the time (I was a retarded twelve) the appearance of the first Anglo-Welsh anthology in 1917 had passed right over my head. And for the next sixteen or seventeen years, that is the period of my adolescence and young manhood in Merthyr and Cardiff, during which my interest in poetry was awakened and my practice of it began, nothing at all seemed to be stirring around me anywhere on the Anglo-Welsh poetic scene. I wrote my first pieces — this was about 1930 — from what appeared the dead centre of a vast poetic wilderness, a sort of silent moon-scape, chilly, twilit, deserted, almost featureless. No wonder one of my earliest verses was 'Maelog the Eremite', a poem about a dotty hermit who came from Merthyr!

And yet it wouldn't be true to give the impression of *complete* inactivity, the idea that nobody at all in Wales at that time was concerned with writing poetry of any sort in English. That's not entirely right. Many young men and women wanted to be thought of as poets — they always do, the supply's inexhaustible. One chap I knew presented me with a selection of his poems which he had typed out, duplicated and bound; another had a volume published by a vanity publisher; two or three, with a lack of reserve I found staggering, openly showed me their poems in thick wads of unpublished typescript. Inevitably I compared this work in my own mind with what I was writing at the time. It seemed to me that the difference between these poets and myself was not really one of talent. It was that I felt profoundly dissatisfied with what I was doing, I knew that in my work there was some indefinable lack, some deficiency, perhaps of vocabulary, some wrongness of mode, or emphasis, or expression. I could see with absolute clarity that most of the work of these acquaintances

67

was written, although they didn't seem to suspect it at all themselves, in an absolutely outworn and exhausted idiom and was concerned with subject matter that had long since, for the time being at least, yielded up its all; that they were composing in a manner utterly incapable of giving shape and vitality to their experiences, assuming that they had any experiences, which in one or two cases seemed questionable. As I say, I couldn't have expressed my dissatisfaction in this way at the time; all I knew was that for some reason this work was, if not absolutely dead, then at least moribund. This conviction of almost complete sterility where writing in English in Wales was concerned helps to explain the tremendous excitement I felt when I first encountered the vitality and the stormy brilliance of Dylan Thomas's early poetry.

One fact I have constantly to adjust to, in talking to people of your generation, is that a good part of my life was over before you were born. So I'd better explain something about South Wales too, because the appalling economic conditions, the poverty prevailing here, the suffering, the hopelessness, had inevitably their effect on the poetic situation. That great Depression of the inter-war years began to be felt in Wales in the Twenties, and the following decade brought to our country a period of unparalleled economic decline and devastation. Closures, widespread unemployment, emigration, extreme and long-term poverty were the agonizing and inescapable features of the time, with disease, bitterness, resentment, and social unrest as the inevitable consequences. Political activity seemed far more urgent to many young people in these circumstances than the unimportant 'fiddle' of poetry. This was the period of the anti-war and anti-fascist rallies, of the great hunger-marches of the unemployed, of the staggeringly successful Left Book Club. The fashionable party then was the Communist Party, not Plaid Cymru. Nationalism to many, to the young Welshmen who fought in Spain perhaps, seemed to have no answer to the ills of Wales, which was suffering in the same way as all the capitalist countries of Western Europe were suffering. What we were witnessing in Wales, as elsewhere, were the dying convulsions of the capitalist system, and the only country, many believed, which had escaped the chaos of the economic blizzard was the one that had already renounced capitalism, namely communist Russia. It's difficult to convey to someone who didn't experience it at first hand the intensity of the sense of frustration and forboding, the despair, the smouldering anger, the passionate rejection, which was then commonly felt by the sensitive young in the presence of so much senseless wastage and suffering and outraged human decency. Hitler at this time also was murdering his way to power in Germany and Mussolini in Italy; the Spanish government was losing its civil war to its own Fascists and the end of democratic Czechoslovakia was in sight. The Second World War, which many believed, ('The bomber will always get through') was to bring western civilization crashing down around us, began to appear as an agonising certainty. Whatever I say about the Anglo-Welsh poets of the Thirties, their problems and their frustrations and their hard-luck, ought to be seen against this appalling background of universal poverty, misery, terror and defeat.

The seventeen years I mentioned just now bring us up to 1934 — I was twenty-nine then — a year important to me personally and in some ways in the history of Anglo-Welsh writing. *The Welsh Outlook* was the only Anglo-Welsh magazine I knew of in the Thirties, which probably means, since I was a relentless hunter-down of such periodicals, that it was the only Anglo-Welsh magazine. (I collected then all sorts of literary and artistic magazines — I wonder how many people still have copies of such hopeful but short-lived publications as *The Islanders, Axis* and *Keltia?*) A monthly, *The Welsh Outlook*, was of general rather than strictly literary interest, more like *Planet*, perhaps, than *Poetry Wales* but its editor did invite contributions "in prose and poetry". In the copies I have here I see articles on 'The Third Reich' and 'An Economist looks at Brynmawr' as well as a translation by Idris Bell of a Rilke poem, a group of seven poems by Huw Menai and an article on the author of 'Y Bardd Cwsc'. The editor, a son of Sir Henry Jones the philosopher, was, among other things, the author of a first-rate escape story of the first World War called *The Road to Endor* — incredible and absolutely absorbing. He had published two or three of my poems and articles over a pseudonym and since he was encouraging and seemed well-disposed towards my work I was hopeful that he might continue to accept further contributions in the future. The sudden end of the magazine in 1934 was a big disappointment. I'd been writing poems for about four years then, in the very discouraging poetic and economic conditions I described earlier, and had already published my work in *The Dublin Magazine, Poetry Chicago* and other 'foreign' journals; but the end of *The Welsh Outlook* meant that no magazine existed any longer in my native country which would publish my poems and the poems of other Welshmen writing in English.

An announcement of the imminent demise of your *Poetry Wales*, would be greeted no doubt by a great outcry throughout the land, perhaps even by a march of protest composed of banner-bearing poets ('Pay Publishing Poets!','Free Cash for Free Verse in Free Wales!') accompanied by their spouses and their pram-borne children, culminating in a chanting sit-in in the offices of the Welsh Arts Council and your publishers. But it would be a grave mistake to suppose that anything like that happened in 1934, that a deafening howl of frustration and protest went up from the Anglo-Welsh poets when *The Welsh Outlook* put up its shutters. In fact there were only three of us. More Anglo-Welsh poets were alive in 1934 of course than just Huw Menai, A.G. Prys-Jones and myself. My researches into the matter — a glance at the contents page of *The Lilting House* — reveal that out of the forty-three poets included in this anthology no fewer than thirty-five, about three-quarters, were in being when *The Welsh Outlook* ceased publication. So, you'll say, what becomes of your claim that you were writing your early poems in a boundless poetic wilderness exhibiting no signs of human habitation? My statement remains true. Because none of the poets born during the ten years following my own birthday had published any poems that I knew of, or any poems at all, by 1934, not Idris Davies, Vernon Watkins, Tom Earley, Brenda Chamberlain, R.S. Thomas, Alun Lewis, Roland Mathias, Cyril Hodges or Keidrych Rhys; or Gwyn Williams, David Jones and Wyn Griffith, all born before me.

But 1934 was the year I first met Dylan Thomas, the year in which the scene, for me at least, began slowly but quite perceptibly to change. Later in that year Dylan published his first book, *18 Poems*. In 1937 Keidrych established *Wales* and one became aware of a further rise all round in the poetic temperature, the first intimations that the ice-cap we had lived with for so long was beginning to retreat. In 1938 Idris Davies published his *Gwalia Deserta*. In 1939 Gwyn Jones founded his *Welsh Review* and my own first volume of poems appeared. In 1941 came Vernon Watkins' *The Ballad of the Mari Lwyd*. A flood of new names, even newer than those of Dylan, Vernon and Idris, began to appear in the magazines — Emyr Humphreys, George Ewart Evans, Ken Etheridge, Nigel Heseltine, H.L.R. Edwards, Lynette Roberts, Margiad Evans, Meurig Walters, Oliver Edwards, and many of these poets I got to know or corresponded with — I am speaking all the time, of course, only of poets. By the outbreak of the second World War in 1939 the first ice age was virtually over.

I dare say a lot of this I've told you many times before. What you might not know is that attempts were made from time to time to render the dreary scene of the Twenties and Thirties a little more friendly, habitable and fruitful — in fact, in the poetic sense, to 'start something'. I mean now the efforts of genuine and knowledgeable poets, not of the rather feeble amateurish writers I described earlier. About 1930, I think it was, I began to discuss with two friends the possibility of starting in Cardiff an entirely *literary* magazine, chiefly for young Welsh people writing in English. We knew of pitifully few such people, only ourselves in fact, but we were hopeful that once our magazine appeared many fine poets, unheard of until then, would proclaim themselves and become our contributors and that large numbers of eager, en-lightened and wealthy subscribers would appear all over Wales and England in the same miraculous fashion. One of my two friends you know, as a frequent contributor to *Poetry Wales* — Elwyn Davies, the author of *Words across the Water*. The other was H.L.R. Edwards, then a student of English at the University College in Cardiff. Harold, now, alas, dead — his end came, oddly enough, on a visit to Naples — was an extraordinary character, a scholar of intimidating range and precision, an uncompromising high-brow, tall, pale, spectacled, bareheaded, a pioneer devotee of the umbrella. I saw him first one night at a table in the reference room of the Cardiff Central Library, the lamplight bright on his Aldous Huxley-like features, engrossed in a reading of *The Apes of God* for which he had managed to forestall me at the counter. One of Harold's hobbies at the time,

Elwyn and I heard with considerable awe, was Chinese; later he certainly became an authority on Stendhal. Although he was really, I suppose, a critic, not a poet, some of his strange, witty verses are to be found in the early numbers of *Wales* — what a contributor he would have made for you, sharp as a needle and always bang up to date! We three, Elwyn, Harold and myself, used to meet to discuss our projected magazine but in spite of our enthusiasm and conviction the only part of our scheme to materialise was the title — *The Broad Arrow*. These words were intended, if I remember correctly, to underline the universality of our magazine's appeal, since they can refer equally to the druidic Three Beams of Light, one of the insignia of the Gorsedd, and therefore of our native Establishment, and also the governmental broad arrows conspicuously branded on the outer clothing of our convicted wrongdoers. What defeated us was a chronic shortage of Welsh cash, Harold being a student supported by his parents, Elwyn working for a pittance as an apprentice journalist and myself a schoolteacher — any further epithet in my case, as you must know, being tautologous.

In one of my early meetings with Dylan he told me that he intended to establish and edit a magazine of poetry and prose to which Welshmen writing in English could contribute. Perhaps you remember reading some account of this project in the introduction to Aneirin Talfan and Ralph Maud's anthology *The Colour of Saying*. Nothing came of Dylan's *Prose and Verse* either, also, I believe, because of lack of available funds. How many other groups or individuals in various parts of Wales were thinking along these lines in the Twenties and Thirties I don't know; the crippling financial conditions prevailing in our country to which I referred earlier probably brought many an enlightened poetic scheme in those years to nothing. Anyway, the first venture of this kind to come to fruition was, of course, Keidrych's *Wales* in 1937. *Wales* accomplished everything we had hoped of *The Broad Arrow* and a good deal more beside.

I think perhaps that other difficulties, apart from the massive financial one, helped to defeat these pioneer editors. One was the fact that they *were* pioneers, absolute beginners with no editorial or business experience to guide them. Another was that no accepted and vitalising Anglo-Welsh tradition, or body of literature, existed behind them or around them, which could act as a stimulus, even as inspiration, to the young writers who might have become their contributors. Also, no-one of outstanding talent, as far as I know, had at that time ever thought of himself as a complete and dedicated Anglo-Welsh poet, or had accepted the role of Welshman committed to his country and her destiny, looking for publication and acceptance in Wales like any of his Welsh-writing compatriots, but yet writing his poems in English. No Anglo-Welsh figure in fact of outstanding achievement and compelling artistic authority had arisen to which the young could look for inspiration, guidance and example — no Yeats, no MacDiarmid. The most famous Welshman writing poetry in English then, I suppose, was W.H. Davies and he, a Georgian, the pet of London super-sophisticates, seemed to lack all the attributes of a likely exemplar. Perhaps Keidrych Rhys himself, aggressive, dedicated, resourceful, contemptuous of the tinsel and intrigue of the London scene, came nearest to being the first true Anglo-Welsh poet. But here in Wales in the Thirties, with our lack of money, magazines, publishers, and audience, and any great successful figure to inspire us, the pull of London was inevitably powerfully felt. London was where ideas were born, where things were started, where contacts were made, where critics lived and where books were published. The early Anglo-Welsh poet has been blamed by some for setting his face so steadfastly towards London and giving only his nape to his own country. But in the circumstances what else could the poor fellow be expected to do?

I've gone on too long. But there's one more thing I must say. From having nothing, we Anglo-Welsh poets are fortunate enough now to have our anthologies of poetry, as well as our individual volumes; we have poetry competitions; records of Anglo-Welsh poetry; poetry magazines; articles, even books, about poets; poetry readings; interest in our manuscripts; even academic attention to our work. Credit for this transformation, whatever explanation modesty might dictate to you, must go largely to the imaginativeness of the Welsh Arts Council's policy towards poetry and literature in general, and the tremendous enthusiasm and skill with which that policy has been carried out by you and the Literature Committee.

One day, when Wales is free and prosperous
And dull, they'll all be wishing they were us,

says Harri Webb. I feel a bit like that too about Anglo-Welsh literature. I wouldn't like to go back to the conditions of the Thirties and I certainly don't wish to suggest that the present poetic scene is dull — far from it. But from this happier present I do look back with a similar sense of perhaps perverse satisfaction at the struggles, the discoveries, the excitements of the past, and at the realisation of the increasing achievement of Anglo-Welsh poetry in the years following 1934.

May the second twenty-one numbers of *Poetry Wales* be even more brilliant than the first. With all good wishes to it, and to you.

Ever,

Glyn Jones

NED THOMAS

A Letter to the Editor

Dear Meic,

I take it that we have at least one preoccupation in common, and that the thought which comes to me from time to time in the course of editing *Planet* must be with you a perpetual and professional concern: are we going to get a great literature out of English-speaking Wales? Have we got the right conditions? Where should one look for the openings? All these questions we ask, I take it, not holding a barometer of national prestige in our hands but because a great literature illustrates (in the Renaissance English sense of 'makes illustrious') the life of a people, and we see the emergence of such a literature as part of the emergence of a people, and of *people*, into a full sense of themselves.

Because particular sections of my book *The Welsh Extremist* provoked the reaction from some people that I as a Welsh-speaking Welshman 'didn't speak for them' let me say that I offer the

74

following thoughts with the question tag 'isn't this so?' and certainly not as some sort of final pronouncement on the situation.

Yes, oh dear yes, the language question raises its head at the very start. I've come to feel more and more since I wrote my book that it is the English-speaking Welshman who is, in the subtler sense, held down in Wales. The Welsh-language situation of crisis confers a kind of dignity on the participants whereas the English-speaking Welshman can easily find himself caught between two kinds of non-acceptance — into the English community and into the Welsh one. The voice which says 'there is a distinct English-speaking culture in Wales to which I belong' is still a weak and uncertain one, and it is kept that way in part by the structure of institutions. An issue such as the future of broadcasting is not unrelated to literature. It may seem propagandistic of me to drag in the Welsh Language Television Channel here, but these things are not unconnected. A Welsh-language channel would mean an English-language channel, and English-speaking Welshmen would be faced with the question of whether *they* wanted 90 per cent of their television to come from London and America or whether they wanted to make more of it here, to deal with our lives. When you create a 'centre' you create the possibility of organizing the dynamic latent in the community that turns in on that centre. I do not want more for Welsh than that it should be given this chance. And I do not want less for English.

I shall not risk predicting the social and political future here. Things work by interaction and what turns out in the end is seldom what anyone expected or intended. But I *do* doubt whether anyone who is unaware of these tensions and possibilities is by today in any real sense experiencing Wales; and any young Welsh writer in English should, I think, clear his mind about these questions.

There are three tenable and honourable positions, it seems to me, and one of these is to leave Wales physically or mentally. It's possible to write about one's experience of metropolitan life for an audience of similar people; it is possible to write in Penrhyndeudraeth a novel about post-atomic-war characters who are seen to be allegorical of blundering man throughout history. But you will have no particular claim on the Welsh public unless you are writing out of some nerve common to you and them.

Or you can stake your life on the notion of a Wales in which everyone will speak Welsh (and English as well). You will see that your children speak Welsh, you will adopt appropriate political positions, and your writing will either show forth the torn condition of your own generation or point the way to the new Wales. Just as the first option robs you of a certain intimacy with the audience in the place where you live, so the second option robs you of the hope of expressing the life of Wales in magnificent and complete and poetic form in the language of your writing; for by your option you imply that complete Welshness will only exist in Welsh Wales, the promised land that you will work for but can never inhabit.

The third choice is a choice in favour of making a culture in English here, now, out of the not immediately promising material. It seems to me that this choice, for it to be an honest one, must recognize that it, too, involves limitations. You are working in a community that has been uprooted, that has been taught to look at itself as provincial, a community where you have no status, that is uncertain of itself, that listens to other voices from other places sooner than to yours, that suffers from an institutional and commercial structure which perpetuates these traits. The odds are against you. But the possibilities are very great. There is a lot to be said for this option, after all. It is the most ambitious one.

I think of the West Indies. What a disastrous background of cultural fragmentation and deprivation! In most places the Spaniards arrived and the Amerindians did not survive. Islands changed hands in wars between the Spaniards, English, French and Dutch. Sometimes the official language changed once a century and the people's language became a jumbled amalgam. And who were the people? Negro slaves brought from Africa, losing their languages, their religion becoming mixed with forms of Protestantism and Catholicism, their lives nasty, brutish and short, continuing in abject poverty for the most part after emancipation. When the negroes left the big estates, the owners brought in contract workers from India. The whites set the negroes and the coloureds (of various shades) against each other, transmitted their own prejudices about pigmentation before taking off in the twentieth century and leaving ex-colonies the prey of world prices for primary products, and of tourism, which turned a popular art form such as the Calypso into an act for the visitor.

The case is an extreme one, but many of the elements are familiar. Like the West Indian we have got used to being seen as objects, as 'Welsh', and lived down to it. This is the terrible truth about power, that it makes the man who has it turn others into objects. Where *he* stands is the centre; *they* stand in relation to that centre. Marvell wrote "Where the remote Bermudas ride/in the ocean's bosom unespied" and it was English poetry exclusively that they read in the schools of the West Indies until recently, so that they were remote to themselves, a speck of red on the map, far flung from the Mother of Parliaments. I noted in my book the way Idris Davies can talk nostalgically and affectionately of "the native language" meaning his own father's language, using *their* word to describe *us*. Reading V.S. Naipaul's *The Middle Passage* I note how *he* notes that a West Indian painter would exhibit a picture of a grass hut on one of their own beaches and call it 'A Native Hut'.

In his introduction to the anthology *Orphée Nègre* Sartre writes: "Here are black men standing, black men who examine us; and I want you to feel, as I, the sensation of being seen. For the white man has enjoyed for three thousand years the privilege of seeing without being seen."

Can't we apply this on a much lesser scale, to ourselves? We have been seen, and when we have climbed into education it has been to see ourselves with *their* eyes. This must be the attraction of the Welsh-speaking culture for any English-speaking Welshman who gets within hailing distance of it — that it is unequivocally *our* account of things and places, and what happened: *Cymru* not Wales, *y werin* not the Welsh peasant-farmers or whatever.

Does this mean that there is no way to become the seer not the seen other than through a separate language? In the ex-British West Indies, especially Jamaica where the African element in the population is large, there is quite an interest in African languages and rather wild notions of relearning them and of going back to Africa. But equally there is successful writing in English, as there is in countries where other languages are strong, for example Nigeria or India. English *can* be wrenched to belong to *us*.

A more homely comparison is to be found in personal relation-ships, where a dominant husband or wife or father or mother makes the other partner in the relationship into the image they have of them; the partner is turned into a thing. If I were writing a short story about such a relationship and I showed the liberation of the dominated partner through his or her sexual assertion of separateness, it would surprise no-one. I wonder how far the analogy can be transferred to a social relationship between groups.

I remember your saying that comparatively few love poems or erotic poems come in to *Poetry Wales*. Little that is good in this field comes in to *Planet* either, though like you I get plenty of statements about Wales in one form or another. Perhaps people think that is what I want. But love is, like nothing else, a centre. It makes here and now the point from which we look out at everything. No wonder the negro's sexuality is feared in the white world. Love humanises places, makes them belong to us:

> But islands can only exist
> If we have loved in them,

writes Derek Walcott from the small West Indian island of Santa Lucia.

From the certainties of love, the sense of filling one's own skin, to knowing where one wants to live, on which corner of the planet one wants to take one's stand, seem small and inevitable steps. Only the good love poet, someone who has found a certainty in himself, could write as Derek Walcott does, taking on himself the immense challenge of submerging himself in a society and encompassing change in the subtle way that is only open to the writer; could reject exile and go for the higher ambition, as the potential great Ango-Welsh writer must:

> I sought more power than you, more fame than yours,
> I was more hermetic, I knew the commonweal,
> I pretended subtly to lose myself in crowds
> knowing my passage would alter their reflection,
> I was that muscle shouldering the grass
> through ordinary earth,
> commoner than water I sank to lose my name,
> this was my second birth.

Yours sincerely,
Ned Thomas

JOHN ACKERMAN

Motor-Mechanic

Sometimes I watch my friend, Ieuan, at work.
Walking where his house leans on the tracked slope
Of a hill, I climb the Autumn pastures,
Finding his yard where our slow machines grope.

Bent over a car, the bonnet up,
Whether a winter wind blisters, cuffing
Down from the mountain sharp blows upon him,
Or summer heat sweats like the oil and grease
His supple fingers charm, strong yet
Subtler than the contours of your scholar's mind,
He advances in all directions against
The dead machine. He does not look up.

I greet him silently, and stand.
His fingers promise life and shrewdly prod
Bearings and plugs, probe the gasket's oily dust.
Here his war on anarchy is fought.
Tracing the engine's lesion, steel's failed nerve,
Habit of inarticulate thought serves
In the give and take against confusion,
Counters the dark mind's slow rust.

"Try it now!" He scolds. The engine throbs. Life
Of a sort stabs the hill's silence. He looks up,
Lighting cigarettes, a patience prodigal and old
As the bare trees burns through our blunt cold.

RHYDWEN WILLIAMS

A Letter to the Editor

(a translation from the Welsh)

Dear Meic,

I've been reading about Solzhenitsyn's Nobel lecture which has just been made available in Stockholm. It is very disturbing.

Did you enjoy the National Eisteddfod? If you had the children with you, you must have done. They see so much and we can always benefit from a child's view. Children speak the truth about life naturally. It becomes more difficult as we grow up.

Once again this year, there seems to be mixed opinion about the Eisteddfod's atmosphere, standards and achievements. Some of its keen supporters I've met have realised for the first time that Pembrokeshire isn't all D.J. and Waldo. One *eisteddfodwr* writing in his denominational paper rejoiced in the fact that he had never met so many Baptists all in one week. The old pride in little kingdoms turned Nonconformist!

I'm looking forward to seeing the next number of *Poetry Wales*. I hope you've had a good response from 'the new poets' and their first appearance in your magazine will inspire them to commit themselves to their "craft and sullen art". For, believe me, the time has surely come for us to take a very serious look at certain aspects of the image and function of the poet in Wales today, especially in the Welsh language.

To begin with, I've been wondering about the old bardic strongholds, — *Eisteddfod Genedlaethol Frenhinol Cymru,* and *Gorsedd Beirdd Ynys Prydain* — and I can't help asking: are they really adequate by now? I ask very earnestly, and — please, believe me — with much appreciation of what has been and still is being achieved, but I am also compelled, like so many others these days, to ponder just what *artistic* role the National Eisteddfod can have in the future.

Take the Gorsedd of Bards — and you'll recall that I've conformed to its ceremony. After viewing the ritual on television

— wide shots, close-ups, and slow pans from druid to druid — I really believe that we must now ask ourselves one or two blunt questions and answer without hiding from the truth behind the Maen Llog. I know the *Werin* love it, but — and I am trying to put this as inoffensively as I can — does it enhance Welsh poetry or is it by now little more than a tourist attraction? As for the Eisteddofod's competitions, is the young poet — Meirion Pennar, Geraint Jarman, Sion Eirian, for example — likely to find 'competition' useful or even attractive? We don't know but I am fairly sure about what it means to them. Furthermore, I would say that the Arts Council in honouring people like Saunders Lewis, David Jones, R.S. Thomas, Kate Roberts, T.H. Parry-Williams and John Gwilym Jones, has given the writer a more dignified position which all trumpets from Llanllechid to Llydaw can never hope to match. As Aneirin Talfan says in the current number of *Y Genhinen*, "By now, the Arts Council is one of the principal patrons of the arts and, with the BBC, of professional artists. The Welsh poet and writer has never had it so good. The Council's annual Prizes make something like nonsense of the Eisteddfod's competitions."

After all, the only test of a poet is his poetry. The gold-plating and finery may be impressive, but they can never symbolize anything other than illusions, half-truths, and pretences. For all the pomp and splendour, a druid remains a druid when he is no longer a poet — and how many on the Eisteddfod stage are poets these days? These symbols, rites, fanfares, regalia, swords, and *hirlas* horns are merely toys made of our conceit and wishful-thinking. While gathering in the charmed circle and exalting grocers, butchers, bankers, policemen, teachers, members of parliament, and musical veterinary-surgeons may be all very well for druids, surely a serious writer can have no time for such make-believe. And what compels me more and more to this conclusion is this: if such fine writers as Williams-Parry, Saunders Lewis, John Gwilym Jones, Gwilym R. Jones, J.M. Edwards, Thomas Parry, Bobi Jones, Alun Llewelyn-Williams, and many others, whose contributions have been so important and whose dedication to Welsh letters so complete, have laboured without attachment to such frivolity, is not the message clear?

For people who honour the poet's skill and calling, I feel more and more that what was staged at Haverfordwest with bugles, prayers, and the strangest costumes outside pantomime is becoming an embarrassment. Old Iolo Morgannwg has had his fun long enough, and in a day when our finest young people are suffering vicious prison-sentences in order that we may be taken seriously as a people, in political terms, I am bound to declare that I think it calamitous that we still present ourselves in such outlandish apparel, and perform a meaningless pageant of platitudes when it is desperately important for our dignity as a nation to be taken seriously in cultural terms too.

One London newspaper sent a reporter to Haverfordwest to take a look at the spectacle. The article that followed was admittedly a bit bold for one who had just floated around for a couple of days, but the inevitable general impression was one of bards, choirs, small-talk, and milk-shakes, an event as light-hearted as a week at Butlin's or the Royal Welsh when it came to brass-tacks. I don't think the bewildered reporter deserved *all* the blame for that impression. How many *eisteddfodwyr* among the 200,000 (or is it 60,000?) attend for artistic reasons?

Aneirin Talfan has asked again in the press — as he had done so many times in the past — just where is the Eisteddfod going? How big is it going to be next time? Few really take notice, for change in the eyes of some *eisteddfodwyr* is irreverence and heresy. And, God bless us, we go on erecting this cultural Taj Mahal in different parts of the country at more and more expense. Good people work hard, talented people rehearse for hours, bards strain in a rhyming tug-of-war, we mourn dead choirs, we welcome lost relatives . . . but we can't honestly say that the event grows better and better, only that it grows bigger and bigger. 'Is there peace?' Yes, plenty, if we are satisfied with false and meaningless ritual and a naive re-enactment of a tradition that never was, an historical leg-pull. Personally, I would prefer a Festival of Wales — with no prizes, no certificates, no preliminaries, no champion recitations, no more *cyd-adrodd,* no adjudicators, no crown bards — but an artistic occasion in the name of the people of Wales to convey, as Solzhenitsyn has just said, "a condensed experience".

Again in Solzhenitsyn's words, writers can help the planet "in its white-hot hour — not by giving ourselves over to frivolous life, *but by going to war*." The way I see it around me today, for whoever would be committed to his craft *as a writer* in Wales now, there can be no peace. There is only war, bitter, prolonged, even violent, through which we must write the truth in the face of all the rotten lies that entangle our lives. Every writer in Wales today is charged with this great responsibility, whatever his language. I believe that sticking to your task as a writer can be as valid an act as going to prison for the language. In a very real sense, writing *is* imprisonment, a life-sentence of hard labour, if we do it properly. There is no room for dressing-up, chanting, and floral-dances in a cell.

So, even if we can't achieve very much, let's join hands with the brave in spirit and the pure in heart.

Cofion cynnes,
Rhydwen

DEREC LLWYD MORGAN

A Letter to the Editor

Dear Meic,

I wish to make a few simple comments on Mr Rhydwen Williams's letter about the National Eisteddfod (*Poetry Wales*, Autumn 1972). A few things in the letter puzzle me. I have failed utterly to see what bearing Solzhenitsyn's remarks can have on the Eisteddfod. Nor can I understand how the parades of the Gorsedd of the Bards can damage the campaigns of *Cymdeithas yr Iaith*. And, by the way, I think it is cold nonsense to compare, as Mr Williams does, the dedication of a writer with the imprisonment of a young Welshman. Another thing, I wish people like Mr. Williams would stop worrying what other nations think of our idiosyncrasies, for this is not the nineteenth century and over there is not the heart of Queen Victoria's empire. Only ignorant men would judge the value of Welsh culture and the dignity of our nation by the cut of the Archdruid's cloak. Does Mr Williams judge Lorca in the light of a bull-fighter's sequins?

Ever since the Welsh, as Frank O'Connor put it, obliged the 'folklorists of the Enlightenment' by inventing 'a few customs for themselves', one of which was the Gorsedd of the Bards, that circle of true and honorary poets has never ceased to be an object of criticism. Gorsedd-baiting was one of our favourite sports at school and college, where we were merely perpetuating a past-time that had been enjoyed by generations of students. Mr Williams does it too seriously.

Our jibes were once taken seriously. In 1963 members of *Gorsedd Môn* were so taken aback by the witticisms of a young college lecturer and a research student whom they had invited along for a talk on their history, that they challenged us students to an *ymryson*. The tournament was held at Aberffraw in 1964, where that grand master of ceremonies, the Reverend William Morris, adjudged our lines to be better than theirs. It is an incident we still talk about. When Llew Llwydiarth threw down the gauntlet in 1963, he acted not as the fool but as a defender of a cult that had given him and thousands of others a great deal of innocent ceremonial pleasure. And pray what is wrong with a bit of colour and pomp? It at least attracts attention to poetry and song. Even Rhydwen Williams brings himself to admit that 'the *Werin* loves it': I hope that is no reason for abolishing it.

The larger Gorsedd of the Bards of the Isle of Britain is for most people the symbol of the National Eisteddfod. And the Eisteddfod in turn symbolizes the vitality of Welsh culture. It is the only national cultural festival that annually affords delight — yes, and infuriating but nonetheless dynamic dissatisfaction — to tens of thousands of Welshmen whose conception of culture would not be maintained if it were done away with. Perhaps that 'conception of culture' is not sophisticated enough for some people — but what of that? If all of us followed the same art fashions we'd make a sorry lot. I know that only a small proportion of Eisteddfodwyr read poetry or sing or study music or stage plays or paint, but merely to benefit in some fashion through contact with such things is rare enough in our day. Any event which fosters such contact should be strongly supported not supplanted.

Eisteddfod Week has become by now a great holiday in the Welsh calendar. For hundreds of families it is what their Games were to Homer's Phaeacians, a festival paid for out of their own pockets and supported by a small fraction of councils' rates, but organized not to dazzle visitors, be they Odyssean or odd, rather to please and excite the natives (all others are very welcome, of course). In this sense the Eisteddfod is indeed a 'watering-place', as I believe Mr Trevor Fishlock called it. Without doubt, psychologically and sociologically, the Eisteddfod has never been more important that it is now.

What I am saying is that Mr Rhydwen Williams's letter is misleading in some ways. The Eisteddfod is not a place where adults do nothing but dress-up. Nor is it just a literary festival held in a charmed circle that 'serious writers' do not enter. The Eisteddfod by now *is* a festival of the arts as well as an organization of competitions. In Haverfordwest last year, for instance, there was a fashion show, an exhibition of paintings, sculpture, clothes, and poetry readings, lectures on censorship, David Jones, Ceri Richards, there was an excellent theatre on the field, and every evening there was a concert in the main pavilion, and two plays in town; and later still *nosweithiau llawen* and discos. What more does one want? All these items of entertainment or whatever were in addition to the daily eight hours of competition in the pavilion. It will be the same in Rhuthun again, as it was in Bangor in 1971.

But it's useless my writing to *Poetry Wales* without saying something about the literary standards of the Eisteddfod. I don't know what point Mr Williams was trying to make when he listed the names of eight writers who did not, or have not, attached themselves to the Gorsedd of the Bards, for it is not the Gorsedd that runs the Eisteddfod. The point worth making is this: of Mr Williams's eight, all have served the Eisteddfod in some capacity, four of them have won either crowns or chairs or prose medals, and all have acted as adjudicators in competitions the winners of which are honoured by the Gorsedd. Furthermore, there is no sense at all in trying to set up a tug of war between the Eisteddfod and the Welsh Arts Council for the honour of 'dignifying' — if I may borrow Mr Williams's word — witers of the standing of Kate Roberts, T.H. Parry-Williams and company. As to Mr

Williams's endorsement of Aneirin Talfan Davies's contention that "The Council's annual Prizes make something like nonsense of the Eisteddfod's competitions", may I ask 'How?' The Arts Council rewards an average of three Welsh authors a year with £300 each (an older, distinguished writer, of course, gets £750), £300 for a book; the Eisteddfod gives 100 for an *awdl* of less than three-hundred lines and another hundred for a *pryddest*: the prose medal winner, I admit, deserves more. Then count the ten and eight pound prizes for lesser poems, and the £50-prizes for essays. I just note these things so that Mr Williams does not kid himself that all the tug is on his side of the rope (that I hope isn't there). I have not said a word about the honour of winning at the Eisteddfod. We'll take that for granted: as John Gwyn of the village grocery did when I came back from Rhos in 1961 with two junior prizes, "You're made now, Der!" he said, and he believed it.

I still have not said a word about literary standards. Sometimes an Eisteddfod produces very good work, sometimes it does not. Standards fluctuate in most fields of human endeavour. Perhaps the best books entered for competition in the last few years are Miss Rhiannon Davies Jones's *Yr Hen Lyfr Cownt*, and her *Lleian Llanllyr*, which justify the holding of dozens of poor competitions. Other novelists, notably Eigra Lewis Roberts and Jane Edwards, have 'graduated', as it were, in National Eisteddfodau. Others have been successful at Urdd Eisteddfodau. Harri Pritchard Jones and Roger Boore, among others, have won prizes for short stories. The gap that existed fifteen or twenty years ago between the Eisteddfodic conception of what good literature was, and the expectations of the more avant-garde critics, that gap has closed. This is a good thing in a way: it has attracted youngsters back to the Eisteddfod stages. But in another way it is sad: I think there is already a Central-Office mentality about the producing of Welsh literature, especially poetry. We need another Gruffydd, a Meuryn too, to watch that we all don't end up writing the same advanced trash. I was just as disappointed as anybody when Euros Bowen's *Genesis* was left unrewarded at Llandudno, but let us not forget that it was the Eisteddfod that attracted his writings in the forties.

With regards to the young poets, about whom Mr Williams is rightly concerned, can he say that a poet will necessarily become a better writer by shunning competition? Does a Lloyd Owen or a Jarman excel just because he competes or does not compete? Competition can be damning; it can also be stimulating. And when a writer chooses to compete incognito under a critic whom he respects, he can do himself a deal of good. Good can come from losing as well as winning. Fortunately there are a few old hands left who have the strength of character to floor a highfalutin' fraud with a generous left hook to the empty head: we need those guys too, and the Eisteddfod used to supply them.

This letter is already too long. I hope Dafydd ap Gwilym has had all the space you had planned for him. To produce a Dafydd ap Gwilym Number of *Poeytry Wales* was an excellent idea.

But to end with Rhydwen. I agree with him only in this, that the Gorsedd of the Bards should not be taken to be a 'true' circle of poets, but they don't regard themselves as such. We would also agree to say that the Eisteddfod should be criticized from time to time, for it is not perfect: it has not been invited to Avallon as yet. I hope all of us will continue to support it, and defend it at all times against the forces that wish to bend its Welsh Rule.

Yours sincerely,

Derec Llwyd Morgan

DAVID JONES

A Letter to the Editor

Dear Meic,

You have asked me to contribute a message of some sort to this issue of *Poetry Wales*, which is composed entirely of critiques of my work over the years. Well, my first duty would seem to be to express my appreciation of you, as Editor, in setting aside a whole issue to this end, and also to indicate my sense of gratitude to the various contributors in considering it worth their time and labour in expressing their personal views in this way.

But I can hardly leave the matter at that, so-to-say, general *Diolch yn fawr iawn*, yet I find it exceedingly difficult to proceed, for to discuss oneself and one's work is beset with complexities, and to employ a familiar analogy, the complexities are 'in depth' and 'along a whole frontage', and having managed to clear one complex of *ffosydd* one finds a 'second line' the rusted entanglements of which present sharp spines of greater embarrassment.

Perhaps all I can do here is to attempt a few chance fragments as they occur to me, that may be indicative of the *nature* of such affinity with the Bret-Weales as I *feel*; and such consanguinity as I have the honour to claim through my father.

It may be possible to indicate something also of my maternal and English side and upbringing. But nothing more than a few remembered or significant fragments is here possible.

Nothing of what Shemus demanded of Shem "from such a year to such and such an hour on such a date at so much a week *pro anno*" is remotely possible, but fragments of a quasi-autobiographical nature intermixt with some of the matters concerning *Yr Ynys hon* that have held my imagination and conditioned my thought since childhood will have to serve.

My father was born in 1860 in Treffynnon and spent his childhood and youth in that town of Gwenfrewi's Well. It is odd to recall that before his coming of age, and totally unknown to his "world of Wales" or the world of England either, in the Tremeirchion area not so very many miles to the west, a 'man in black' entranced by the particular characteristics of Welsh metric was at his labours which were destined within half a century to have a very decided effect on English *poiesis*. The mere idea would have seemed as impossible in Sir Fflint as it would have seemed preposterous and outrageous to *The Times* newspaper.

Governmental English opinion and anglophile Welsh opinion in the eighteen-sixties and 'seventies are sufficiently well known, so that the suggestion that this Brittonic tongue, "the main obstacle to civilization in Wales", could ever, under any circumstances, be a vivifying influence on English poetic forms would have appeared not much less absurd than to suggest a revival and vivification of *yr iaith Gymraeg* itself.

But we all tend to suppose of something or other that we think long since ploughed-in and forgot that "the dew on him did fall . . . and Barleycorn stood up again and that surprised them all!"

My grandfather, John Jones, and I think his wife also, were natives of Ysgeifiog, which place is on or very near the presumed alignment of Clawdd Offa. I say presumed because while that remarkable earthwork is fully evident to archaeologists some miles to the south and picks up again nearer the coast, there is a gap in the evidence in the Ysgeifiog area of Tegeingl. I write from a Nursing Home and so am without the requisite maps and references, so write as my memory serves. But John Jones, Ysgeifiog, has always been associated in my mind with the great vallum of the Mercian King in the 8th century, which looks one way toward the Welsh heartland and its hills and thick wooded valley-ways, and beyond to the heights of Arfon herself, while the other way, looking east lay the flats and richer soil of what was to become shire-land of the Mercian — deep-furrowed of the coulter, wider the share's furrow of the heavy English plough-beam.

It appears John Jones Ysgeifiog, although totally Welsh in blood, and who habitually conversed with his wife in the native tongue, discouraged, as far as he could, the use of Welsh in his eldest son, my father. His other children appear to have used either tongue as they chose. It is easy to see the intention of John Jones, it was to make his eldest son as fully English-speaking as may be. How else 'get on' in the world?

It reminds one of those stern warnings of 16th century Welsh gentry, who in sending their sons to Oxford, bade them refrain from using Welsh even to their intimate Welsh friends and roommates, but to speak only and at all times in English, the tongue of the Queen's realm. Coleg Iesu, Rhydychen, was hardly intended to foster the tradition of the 'carpenters of song', the *seiri cerdd* of the *colegau barddrin*.

'The Silky One' they called her, schooled on the lap of Pallas Athene, would have the young gentlemen of Our Dominion of Wales look to a Sibyl very other from those tutelaries that had sustained the *uchelwyr* and *bonheddwyr* in their lime-whited enclosures — not so very different from *Y Dref Wen* at the confines of the green *coedwig* recalled in the Heledd saga of 9th century Powys. For though the metamorphoses in the life of the Cymry were indeed very many and increasingly erosive, yet down through the intervening centuries there still echoed the *cerdd* of nearly a millennium back.

Taliesin, Aneirin, a Talhaearn called 'Father of the Muse' of immediately sub-Roman Britain. And the *chwedlau* of the tale-tellers, how else the *mabinogi* of the Four Branches? How else the stupendous story of the hunting of the Boar Trwyth? Or indeed of all that baptized complex coming to us from a common Celticity of pre-history, hence with Irish parallels? Or the Dream of Macsen Wledig, recalling our Romanity? It is crucial to remember that, alone of the peoples of this island, the leaders of the Bret-Wealas arose from within the Western Xtian imperium.

It may seem a very far cry from the great border families such as the Vaughans or the Herberts in the reign of Elizabeth the First to the humble families of farming stock or craftsmen of the Clwyd or Dee in the reign of Victoria, but their motives were not all that dissimilar.

John Jones wished his son to be at no disadvantage in the great world, so the more the lad had command of English, the better. But of course it was impossible to be brought up in Treffynnon in the eighteen-sixties and seventies without an understanding of *yr hen iaith* alongside the speech of 'the children of Ronnwen', the tongue of the burgess breed of 'the daughters of Alis', the tongue of the Realm of our sovereign Lady Victoria.

But was not she 'exalted with the Crown of London', like Bendigeidfran son of Llyr?

Kleio plays her own tricks.

My father knew and could converse in Welsh along with his play-mates, though it *may* be not with the fluency of his younger sisters and brothers, in that they were, it seems, exempt from any parental discouragement. A curious case of primogeniture, applied to linguistics, in gavelkind-minded Wales.

But I do not know enough of the actual situation to speak with any confidence, but am judging from subsequent fragments of evidence.

My father had come to London in the eighteen-eighties and by the time of my childhood in the first decade of this present century, if his Welsh was greatly eroded, he sang songs to us in Welsh, and the clear-vowelled Cymraeg and perfect pitch without any sign of effort filled me with wonder, certainly with pride, and a kind of awe. He also told us stories current in that north-eastern corner of the Welsh lands from which he had come. It was that sense of 'otherness' that was the heritage he handed on to me.

I have no forgetfulness of being taken for the first time to visit relatives in Gwynedd Wen.

Somehow or other we were packed into a hansom, two parents, three small children and much impedimenta, to Euston for the night-train, so it was pitch dark for most of the journey. I was fast asleep and can remember nothing until we were, I suppose, somewhere between Crewe and Chester, anyway it was, I think, light, but I was told to go to sleep again as there was a long way yet to go. Somewhere west of Chester I was again wide awake, and my father was saying, "Well, here you are now, or will be in a few moments". I looked one way and the coastal flats of the wide estuary of the Dee stretched to the taut line of the sea-horizon. I looked the other way along the *morlan* to the rising contours of the hills and far beyond them in the morning light the misted heights, now lost, now found, away to the fastnesses of Gwynedd Uchaf. Though of course I had not yet heard that term. But the Rubicon had been passed. And so this was the land of which my father had so often spoken and that's why he had said just then, "Well, here you are now".

This was at least the first glimpse of a visual 'otherness' and for me it was an otherness that, as is said of certain of the sacraments, is not patient of repetition, but leaves an indelible mark on the soul of us.

Yours sincerely
David Jones

JOHN BEYNON

Billiard Hall

Down a breakneck flight
Of scuffed steps
From the crowded street
Where shoppers queued
At bus stops, chatted, paid bills,

91

Spent normal lives,
The billiard hall
Malingered in the gloom.
Tables supported
Rectangular blocks of dirty light,
Whilst between and around

Were corridors of dark
Where the flotsam of the town
Found refuge from sunshine
That was too bright,
From rain, from cold.
I knew them all, by sight:
Jack 'the Rob' who never worked,
Enemy of the Welfare State,
Who stepped aside to hide
From the taunting spectre of a job;
The brothers Sid 'n Sam

Who lived on Kilvey
In a shack, kept chickens,
Shot rats for fun, lied;
Old Stickey and Fergus,
Oddjob men who were
Always at each other's throats,
The best of pals;
Childmen on leave from hospital
For the afternoon,
Unable to fathom
The strongbox of the Mind . . .

And others who in spring
Saw the vivid balls
Flower on the evergreen nap,
Summer, Autumn, Winter
Until the mean day died
With a sudden metallic Snap!
They were soon lost
In the cellars of the night,

Penumbra men who took no cue,
Chalked up no scores,
Were neither good nor kind,

Frequently obscene as they
Failed to pocket
The petty thievery of their ways,
But rebounded crazily
From side to side,
Were spun, screwed, smacked,
Red and green and black and blue,
Made no breaks, shot no pools,
Were snookered from the start
And could not play
Unless they broke the rules.

SHEENAGH PUGH

Spring

Now open flowers on the shirts of boys;
now mica glistens, asphalt's morning dew,
from pavements up. Now all the girls look pregnant,
and small red sports cars blossom on the roads.

Now all birds are not sparrows; now all women
unwrap their shapes from winter. Now the man
who thought it might be fun to walk to work
finds all sight aches, all touch troubles his blood.

Now all the state of opening, upspring, bud's
soft burst, a green grenade, scrapes at his grief;
now all the many dead dress him in black
for what they had and what he cannot keep.

R. GEORGE THOMAS

Dylan Thomas And Some Early Readers

Who were his early readers? There can be no final demonstration or proof of the exact size or composition of a poet's audience at any given time; critical acclaim, the rapid issue of editions, or press notices are weak indications of the amount of poetry actually read and repeatedly re-read. What follows here is an attempt to indicate the taste and expectation of the audiences to whom I introduced Thomas's early verse before 1945. During the thirties Thomas never appealed to the politically conscious reader who read and supported the Left wing magazines; but not all readers of the Left wing poets condemned Thomas's verse or his experimental methods. Many undergraduates welcomed his oddness and obscurity because it showed a clear refusal to write like the Georgians, or the Tory-Christian Eliot. Thomas's apolitical attitude was deplored, even while his manner of writing was approved, because it reflected a sense of chaos and helped to chart one of the many paths leading towards an impending 'Day of Judgement'. There could hardly have existed in large numbers any such mythical monster as a purely Left wing reader of poetry. The few that I met, during the time of the Spanish Civil War, rejected vehemently the poetry of the Oxford pink poets of the Left. Thomas's verse was read with reservations by this special audience of the politically committed, but they did read him and they provided a considerable part of the intellectual ferment of South Wales. Nor would the praise of Dr. Edith Sitwell have helped the poet's reputation at that time with this kind of reader. The Indian summer of her reputation as a poet and publicist almost coincided with Thomas's own post-war reputation. Quite possibly the one assisted the other in England, as it most certainly did in the U.S.A. Admittedly these are hazardous conjectures because all such opinions rest on unscientific guesswork muddled with hindsight, though borne out by jottings I made at 'question time' on the notes of lectures I gave between 1936 and 1945.

Perhaps this cloud of supposition about the pre-war reception of Thomas's poetry can be clarified by considering the reputation of two other South Wales writers during the same period. The cogent fact of the war-time reputation of Alun Lewis is one tangible piece of evidence. In the few years before the War their poems could be found side by side in the same magazines. They were of an age and came from the same kind of South Wales family background. Neither spoke Welsh and while Lewis was himself a graduate, Thomas had many graduate or student friends. Both, like so many other writers then, avoided writing for the stage, the radio, or the novel: they concentrated on non-narrative poetry and short stores that derived considerable assurance — if no conscious assistance — from D.H. Lawrence, James Joyce and, possibly, Chekhov. Rilke and Kafka were known to both of them and for each marriage became a powerful healing force that affected their writing, visibly and unmistakably. Before he died in India the disciplined and sensitive clarity of Alun Lewis's awareness of the world of personal relationships was giving his verse a sharper edge — even as he recoiled from violence — and was impelling him towards story writing and the novel. His death near the Burma border was a public event reported in *The Times*; his verse was accepted by Service readers as a true report of a soldier's life — but it made no powerful impact on the immediate post-war generation. For my present purpose, the significance of Lewis's sudden blaze of war-time fame lies in its not being accorded to Thomas. Lewis's work could have been accepted for its manner and matter in any of the pre-war and war-time journals: he was recognisably 'of the period' in a way that Thomas was not. Yet Lewis found *his* manner at the very time that Dylan Thomas was shaping and writing his own most authentic poetry.

Alun Lewis was not particularly fond of subjects with a genuine 'Anglo-Welsh flavour'. To me, and to people like me at the time, this absence of Welsh flavour was not a defect. We were much clearer about what were *not* acceptable subjects for poetry than we were about the necessary areas of experience that could (or should) be exploited in verse. Without any falsification I think I can recall the demands of young readers in those days as a demand for honesty of manner, tone and *weltanschauung*. Auden, Spender, Day Lewis and MacNiece were considered less effective in their marching songs than in the analyses of their personal

dilemmas, which we all shared. There was, of course, a conspiracy against our elders who had survived from *their* War into
what was rapidly becoming ours, particularly those writers who
still wished poetry to be identified with the verse of the Georgian
week-enders. Even Yeats's reputation was not shock-proof against
the enthusiasm of younger readers for Wilfred Owen, Edward
Thomas and Isaac Rosenberg. In a similar way, much of the poetry
of Pound, Eliot and G.M. Hopkins was acceptable to us only when
it seemed to fit the current need for 'honesty above everything'.
So those present-day scholar-critics who expect the poetry of
Thomas and Lewis to have voiced the social unrest of a depressed
South Wales are making demands of the poetry that were rarely
made by the contemporaries who first read their verse.[1]

Another Welsh writer, Idris Davies (known then as the author
of *Gwalia Deserta*), actually did use the social and economic
decay of an old, early Industrial Revolution iron-town as a
background theme for his thin and bitter minor verse. But in
those days I noted (in a review) that the subject and not the poet
was contributing a living quality to *his* verse: his minor voice
remained as an honest attempt to state clearly what had been
experienced too rawly for transmutation into poetry. Thomas and
Lewis, unlike Idris Davies, had never worked as miners, had
never lived in miners' cottages, had never been unemployed or
'on the dole', had never been cramped in by Miners' Institute
Marxism on the one hand and Calvinistic pulpitology on the
other. In this respect they were as free as air and they chose the
subjects of their poetry accordingly. Idris Davies *had* to write
about what he knew — the social and economic decay of
Rhymney. It was only an accident that a few Oxford poets, who
were also free to choose their own subject, had, for some obscure
reasons[2] chosen this same topic of the economic run-down of the
old-fashioned side of British industry as a dynamic theme in their
own revolutionary verse. There was, we felt, a strong element of
guilt, as well as a touch of social conscience, in the verse of these
English poets of the middle class. By contrast, Thomas and
Lewis, brought up in the almost class-less society of Swansea
and Aberdare, shared no such guilty feelings because, in their
different ways, they had not been separated by education or social
stratification from an intimate contact with the broken lives

around them. If my own parallel experience is anything to go on, the absence of any opportunity of employment in South Wales left young students free to indulge in their personal development as writers without the need for social involvement; the idleness of a community on the dole encouraged a self-absorption in a world of the imagination which lay readily to hand in books, in argument, in music and abundant physical leisure. Although his economic condition was much more desperate than ours, even the much harder pressed Idris Davies felt no call to political action of any kind: the conditions of the time seemed to encourage fantasy and escape — and he indulged it.

The febrile grotesqueness of this decade between 1930 and 1940 was accurately mirrored for me in Dylan Thomas's verse. Some critics have fastened on a feverish quality in his earliest poems and have subjected them to the most faithful explication in sexual terms. This is an odd pre-occupation. Most of us can recognise the dirt: we have all been schoolboys, undergraduates, soldiers and readers of Elizabethan and Restoration drama; James Joyce had not passed our way unheeded. What amazes me about some critics of *18 Poems* and *25 Poems* is that they recognize the sex symbols but ignore the world of fantasy and nightmare out of which the poems developed. Even rarer is the critic who pays much attention to the experiences of the youthful Thomas as a cub reporter for a local newspaper in a town that was also a port in the depths of the South Wales economic depression. The public morgue and not the public bar seemed a more likely source for much of this young poet's bizarre view of the world. The curiously local standard of a local newspaper, with its conscientious neglect of the main items of world news and its studious concentration on the twisted slant given to ordinary respectable behaviour, is a partial explanation of the ease with which Thomas's earlier prose (and his later script-writing) came to rely on the salacious event and the outrageous incident in order to gain a quick effect.

One of the first poems to appear in an anthology was *The force that through the green fuse drives the flower*. As many readers recognized then, the confused and horrible images in the last verse of this poem were acceptable not as good reportage but as an externalized expression of long supressed fantasies and fears:

The lips of time leech to the fountain head;
Love drips and gathers, but the fallen blood
Shall calm her sores.
And I am dumb to tell a weather's wind
How time has ticked a heaven round the stars.

And I am dumb to tell the lover's tomb
How at my sheet goes the same crooked worm.

If I recall my contemporaries' reactions accurately, this poem was not sifted and weighed in the fine balances of semantic analysis in search of symbolic significance or sexual double-talk. It was accepted as a fairly clear realization of unknown sources of physical suffering that must lie ahead of us, most probably in gas warfare or Guernica-like devastation. None felt uneasy about the macabre images in the poem, though all detected the mixed attitudes of confident exhilaration and wry acceptance of fate that were conveyed, without intellectual resolution, in the poem's tone and rhythm. There was a nightmare quality in the drift towards Hitler's War which was echoed more closely in Thomas's non-political verse than in any of the Home Guard poems of C. Day Lewis or the twisted agonies of Spender's more personal verse. Thomas actually never joined the body of war-time writers who tried to band themselves in Apocalyptic union; but the fact that the Apocalyptic poets claimed his allegiance is a fairly clear pointer to one way in which his poetry was being read in the late nineteen-thirties and forties.

The drift of this argument seems to suggest that I often presented Thomas to audiences as a journalist in verse. When Vernon Watkins published Dylan Thomas's letters to him, the chorus of public reviewers sang in unison on one theme: the letters were disappointing in any insight they might have given into the poet's own attitude towards his "craft and sullen art" or, indeed, into his opinion of the work of other poets, including the major English writers. There was little need for Thomas to show off his knowledge of literature to Vernon Watkins or to his other close friends from his early formative days. They met too frequently to be ignorant of such things. The letters, then, became footnotes to a text which can never be printed. Other writers have turned to Thomas's broadcast talks for evidence of his literary knowledge: surely, a fallacious proceeding which confuses the image of the young poet with that of the public figure and script writer. This dedicated investigation into Thomas's 'literary sources' reflects some genuine confusion about the state of the criticism of poetry in England before and after the Second World War.

Thomas, I know, was at first genuinely puzzled when he was expected to enter into long correspondence with research students about the explication of his verse. He could be ribald, offhand and mischievous on the subject. Yet his basic attitude to such critical enquiry was not wilful. He assumed that his task was to make his poetry as clear as he could and, to this end, the young poet worked hard in the only way he knew — he polished and excised and re-wrote draft after draft. When his job was done, the reader was expected to take over without any possibility of back-tracking to earlier versions or intentions.(If I understand correctly what he said — in long discussions after three lecture-visits paid to our English Department — his ultimate concern was to find a significant form for each poem. One of my notes states him as saying "When I have finished a poem, the last version is the only poem I want read".) Since 1950 the habit of analysing poetry has become as much an academic chore and escape-hatch in England as it was in America in the 1930's and '40's. The combined effect of I.A. Richards, of *Scrutiny*, and the New Criticism has created as big an audience for books and articles *about* modern literature as there are readers of new writing in little reviews and ephemeral publications intended for the avant-garde. Nevertheless, the economics of publishing and the now academically respectable pastime of keeping ahead in one's fashionable literary taste, should not be allowed to obscure the quite different relationship that existed between poet and reader when Dylan Thomas was shaping his best verse. For war-time England was, if anything, even more favourable to readers of poetry than the 1930's: magazines were easily posted to soldiers and were readily available on railway bookstalls. Servicemen had a great deal of off-duty time to spend with little money for spending: reading was a widespread occupation.[3] Again, too much can be made of the fact that *18 Poems* was published because Thomas had won a poetry competition with these poems in a popular Sunday newspaper.

A few hours spent reading the back files of now defunct dailies of the 1920's and 1930's should convince the most hardened sceptic that, before the War, the personal literary taste of the editorial board could be indulged with considerable latitude before the charge of 'long-haired' (or 'highbrow') was raised against them in the interests of the 'common' (or 'lowbrow') reader.

From 1920 until the war-time 40's there existed many magazines and reviews that published a great deal of poetry as well as short stories, features, and some book reviews, on the assumption that poetry was part of the tasteful entertainment of the average reader. Long articles of literary criticism, devoted almost entirely to the evaluation or elucidation or sociological unravelling of verse or prose, were much rarer then than they are today in our dwindling number of weeklies, monthlies and quarterlies. The energies of the higher journalism of distinguished academic writers before the War were devoted largely to the elucidation of long-dead writers. The sharp contrast with the habits of today needs no underlining here: but it is necessary to be aware of the change in order to understand the climate of approval in which Thomas wrote his earlier verse. There are many shorthand ways of expressing this pre-war relationship between poet and public:[4] 'the poet viewed himself as a seer'; 'he retained the egocentric conception of the Romantic legislator'; 'his poetic activity was a near-religious act blasphemously conceived as a kind of revelation'; 'the poet was a necessary, neurotic scape-goat for the ills of a declining (or sinful) civilization'. In other words, before the War the ordinary reader did not expect a poet to conform to any single pre-conceived political or critical conception of what his poetry be like — or what elements it should contain.

In this common eclectic attitude towards the name and nature of poetry — shared by readers and writers alike — lies the source of Thomas's puzzlement when it was made clear to him that some post-war critics expected him to have been more careful with the superficial 'prose meaning' of his poems. My generation, that had swallowed *The Waste Land* at the beginning, *Ulysses* (when available) in the middle and, with some difficulty, *Finnegan's Wake* at the end of a twenty-year period of literary experiment, had somehow learned to take a great deal of obscurity along with its entertainment. The 'advanced' reading public, in particular,

100

had learned to allow considerable latitude to the writers: like the painters, sculptors and musicians, poets were credited with knowing what was best for their special public. The reaction to this latitudinarian attitude since 1946 has been hostile and, on occasions, quite school-marmish. Nowadays the interpreter (or the critic) seems to know best. But this new emphasis on formal clarity has been accompanied by a decline in the general bill-of-fare provided by weekly journalism for the 'common reader' and a catastrophic shrinkage in the size of the reading audience of avant-garde publications. I believe that Thomas found it much easier to cross the border from writing poetry to writing for the entertainment world, because, before the War, he had never felt the need to recognize the existence of such a frontier. The poet of *18 Poems* and *25 Poems,* the prose and verse writer of *Map of Love,* the author of *Portrait of the Artist as a Young Dog,* represent different sides of a young writer who seemed to know the conflicting imaginative needs of the same kind of reader. The yawning gap that exists between the poems of *Deaths and Entrances* and the script of *Under Milk Wood* is a measure of Thomas's awareness of a fragmentation of literary culture that had taken place between 1940 and 1953. Not to credit him with this awareness — however much one might like to deplore his exploitation of the new cultural situation — is to under-estimate one significant sanction for his earlier 'obscurity' of manner when he was trying both to shape his poetic medium and to define the precise areas of experience within which his poetic statement could be most clearly made.

Thomas himself smudged an important part of the distinction between his early and later verse when he wrote, in the Note to *Collected Poems,* that his poems "with all their crudities, doubts, and confusions, are written for the love of Man and in praise of God, and I'd be a damn' fool if they weren't". Two attitudes are implied here: a war-time religiosity which seemed to spread into many public utterances from the time of the 'miracle of Dunkirk' onwards, and a pre-war intellectual attitude of disregard for (rather than hostility towards) the claims of religious belief upon the artist and the writer. I really am in no position to comment on the existence of Christian belief among the post-war poetry reading public: I can however record the fact that the publication of Eliot's *Four Quartets* has forced literary critics to give much more attention to Christian teaching and dogmatics than was thought possible (or desirable) among Welsh undergraduates or scholars in the inter-war years. Jesus, the social teacher and soul (or psyche) healer, was then a more dominant figure in literary discussions than Christ, the founder of a living Church with its own dogmatics. While it is easy to produce a roll-call of Christian writers who were active between 1926 and 1940, I cannot remember that, outside the circle of believers, such consciously Christian writers were then considered to form the main stream of English writing. The active interest among young people in the work of Joyce, Virginia Woolf, D.H. Lawrence, Pound, Rilke and Kafka gives some idea of the vague interest shown towards Christian apologetics by the majority of magazine readers. Marxism, with its materialistic basis; the various schools of psychology, with their apparent disapproval of the existence of a soul; these were some of the fashionable topics of loose discussion which, one thinks, can be seen to underlie Thomas's short stories and his thinly-veiled autobiographical writings before the War. Yet, in his verse Thomas seemed to take Bible Christianity quite seriously. This is a difficult and complex subject, particularly because some of the exaggerated claims made for him as a religious poet are based on poems drawn indiscriminately from all periods of his writing and few of his expositors understand the particular nature of Nonconformity in Wales as a contributory factor to any uninstructed Welsh Christian's thinking. Thomas's *Note* has its own confused and doubtful crudities of expression, not the least of which is the almost truculent face-saving conditional clause with which it ends. This clause robs the whole statement of any positiveness and, to my mind, places his attitude to religion back in the thirties, but with an added note of awareness of supernatural events which was absent from his earlier Darwinian-centred verse and which followed on from his own war-time ponderings on birth, marriage, and death. He would not be the first artist of his generation who, in the post-war world, tried to find some personal formula that would reconcile the conflicting claims that had been made upon his developing personality by the advocates of Communism and Christianity. This much is certain: among the younger non-Christian poets writing before 1940, Thomas was most noticeable for his constant use of what I can only term 'Bible-Christianity'. One remembers that his great-uncle was a Welsh Baptist poet-preacher with Unitarian leanings: but that isolated fact scarcely warrants a use of the term 'Christian' to describe Dylan Thomas the young poet.

No picture of Thomas in his formative years can be adequate without some recognition of the influence upon him of the poetry of G.M. Hopkins and the shadow of Yeats's reputation and practice. The evidence of Hopkins's influence was plain to all who knew the poet before the War: he knew by heart long extracts from Hopkins's poetry and would declaim 'The Leaden Echo and the Golden Echo' with considerable fervour and self-abandonment. In the '30's, the fashionable interest in, and critical comment on, Hopkins's poetry was concentrated on the form and the rhythm: readers and lecture audiences, I found, were less interested in the implied theology. Thomas was no exception and I believe that the practice of Donne and Hopkins gave him the sanction he required to make his own half-colloquial use of Christ's name in his own verse: it surely supplied him with the "in praise of God" phrase in the *Note* to his *Collected Poems*. The letters to Vernon Watkins suggest the powerful effect of Yeats's verse upon him at a time when there was no easily accessible collected volume of Yeats's poetry. The example of Yeats was a significant one. At all times Thomas was very shy on this subject of being a full-time, dedicated poet and the portrait of him acting as a poet-buffoon in America would seem to rob what I now have to say of its validity, if a careful distinction is not drawn between the various public images of Dylan Thomas that the public entertainer, Dylan, helped to foster. Up to 1940 Thomas believed that the artist could live in and on the community, without losing his self-respect, in exchange for complete dedication to the artist's craft. This genuinely shy man was capable of holding convictions with fanatical intensity and Yeats, whom he knew of by hearsay, and Augustus John, whom he knew more intimately, were two examples, that he occasionally cited, of artists who had found their proper place in society. Thomas was no scholar, but he was an avid reader of miscellaneous works that interested him. He read widely in the Caroline divines, for example. Consequently, no thorough academic reconstruction of the influence of Hopkins's and Yeats's writings upon his work can be much value as a guide to their effect on his development. He used them as though they were his contemporaries — and therefore, his equals — to be chewed over, criticized or admired; and certainly to be absorbed into his system like nourishment, because of their confidence and their successful resolution of artistic problems. In particular, I think, both Hopkins and the later Yeats confirmed Thomas in his intense concentration on the task of producing a significant form for each separate poem, as the correct manner in which a twentieth century poet should communicate with his readers. (Joyce's example in prose was another frequently approved writer that Thomas cited in this connection.)

This attempt at a reconstruction of the nature of an audience's interest in poetry and its expectations from a young poet in the 1930's has not been undertaken in order to prepare the ground for a *Bildungsroman* of Dylan Thomas. It is still too soon to make definite pronouncements about the poet's stature: had Yeats died even as late as 1918, he would hardly have counted as more than a minor poet in the history of this century's literature. If Thomas's eventual niche is alongside poets like Smart or Beddoes, the heavy superstructure of a full-scale study would soon topple over. But the conditions under which he attempted (and achieved) his own kind of poetic statement need to be re-called now that modern poetry is, on the one hand, almost a private academic game and, on the other, part of a growing, commercial entertainment industry. For Thomas wrote when, despite notable casualties, there were still magazines in England , Ireland and Wales that presupposed a reading public which faintly resembled the pre-1914 social conditions of literature — when the writer and his reader felt themselves to be on equal intellectual and social terms. In the 1930's, young men with quite small private incomes could set themselves up as full-time professional writers, and even as publishers. Such conditions placed a premium on the young artist's personal search for self-realization — and encouraged that quest. Thomas had no private income but, until his marriage, he could rely on some financial support from his parents; part of his personal tragedy in the last decade of his life seems to derive from his inability to come to terms with the vastly changed economic situation of would-be professional poets after the War. But such considerations are irrelevant — or, more accurately, external — to any assessment of his poetry which was hammered out in the completely different pre-1940 atmosphere in an almost prison-like solitude. In my early advocacy of Thomas's *Deaths and Entrances* in lectures given to some post-war university audiences, I was frequently asked to defend Thomas's verse against the charge of 'wilful misuse of the English language'. This article is an attempt to show why Thomas really believed that he had sufficient sanctions for all the experiments he was trying to make in his early verse. What seemed 'wilful' to some critics, was to him the most natural and most expected of all ways of writing, and therefore needed no extra-poetic justification. The argument becomes confused after 1946, when Thomas tried to maintain a precarious balance between the profitable role of public entertainer and his earlier habit of solitary, hermit-like poetic composition. The result, in personal terms, was a tragedy for his family, his friends and himself, but his early death and its public nature, together with the freak success of *Under Milk Wood,* has obscured the partial success with which the later Dylan Thomas was striking a new balance in his verse between the claims of entertainment and personal poetic statement. The explication of this theme is another matter. As far as I know, it has not been successfully attempted so far.

Notes

1. Because this is a kind of sociological report, it begs the vital question of 'who does a poet write for?'
2. Obscure, that is, to the men I lectured to in between 1936 and 1940 in Miners' Institutes in South Wales.
3. Grammar school boys entering the Services usually read more widely in literature than they would normally have done in peace-time when they would have spent their leisure either in sport or practical amusements or in utilitarian career studies.
4. I am referring here to the average reader of literature I met and lectured to in literary societies. Literary historical criticism is, I believe, already hardening into an orthodoxy whereby Eliot, Richards and Leavis are accepted as the standard interpreters of the inter-war years and not, say, Middleton Murry, Charles Morgan, V. Woolf. or de la Mare.

TONY CURTIS

Chat Show

You've got it made:
they hang to your pauses,
the questions your host feeds to you.
Because you're

THE MAN

A few easy openers about the early days,
how you began;
the vaudeville act with your sister
— you supporting her.
        Then
the move to broadway, the shows, films.

Feint surprise as he asks you to sing;
'Cheek to Cheek'
'Putting on the Ritz'
        — applause each time.

But
    when, larger than life, your image
fills the screen behind you,
top hat, tails and cane weave a memory.

        That
is the real thing:
the breathless grin,
hands waving like a magician's;
            feet

machine-gunning the beat
as if the hands held strings.
You vault chairs and tables;
piano and bar are props around which
you spin the number.

Finally, as all had anticipated,
he coyly challenges you to dance.
        At
seventy, wrinkled neck like bark,
you take the cue.
        The band's plushness
now serves to cover the dulled edge of your tapping.

Satisfied, the audience applauds
the length of the credits;
was worth the price to say:

      'I saw Astaire dance.'

      They
carry the movie image home in their minds,
nostalgic tunes all the way,
blind to the varicose veins, ignoring the toupé.

JOHN DAVIES

Sunny Prestatyn

Each day I see them carefully grow old and feed
    behind that glass, those plants,
in an aquarium's stillness — saw at first their need
    for aloneness like a niche.
It is not a need. Lured by sun-crossed memories
    of August, most have retired
from industrial towns at last to find the sea
    sucked out of reach.

They have left the wet streets that flow
    on Northern towns like tides,
those separately secret worlds that tow
    forever in their wake

lives bound by the going and returning they inhabit,
    for this quiet place
where silent mornings on the daylight hours sit.
    Here no tide will break.

Some watch the sand, the blank sea stretching out, going
    endlessly nowhere.
Past bungalows, an empty paper bag goes yachting
    down the empty street.
Cars pass; seagulls stream on white safaris to the sea.
    Like their bungalows,
the old here are detached, with no shared memory
    to sift or curse or greet.

And if they had known of this, would they have stayed
    where home and friends
still were, where the family was once, and made
    the most of their discharge?
Anywhere, lack of interest, change and age itself condemn
    them, left on some beach
or trapped in tanks. We are accused of them
    and they are us writ large.

PETER ELFED LEWIS

Yes, And Even You, Thomas Carew

The Cavalier poet speaks to a modern American girl in Los Angeles.

Come strip, my love, your clothes unfurl,
    Your wobbly breasts uncover,
Come rip your panties off, my girl,
    And then we'll joys discover.

Unzip your blouse, unsnap your bra,
    Unslip your nylon slip,
Be ready for our supine spar
    And my Samsonian grip.

Kick off your shoes with ten inch heels,
    Unclip your Dior stockings,
Then we'll to bed with sighs and squeals
    And cease unchaste defrockings.

Yank off your swanky, yankee skirt,
    Roll off your rigid roll-on,
Before I roll on you, sweet flirt,
    Deriding sinless Solon.

Now kiss me with your ten inch mouth
    As large as Moby Dick's,
For fickle I must travel South
    When I have had my kicks.

So with your winding legs entwine,
    O Octopa, my carcass,
Bestride me in a wry design,
    Caress my care-worn corpus,

And swallow, with my tongue and lips,
    My pyrotechnic passion,
Which grips your all, e'en slippy hips,
    And yields your flesh love's ration.

Dear pet, there'll be no petting now,
    No stateside innovations,
We'll act the risqué play, I vow,
    Without your reservations.

I'll seek that stronghold of all maids,
    Besiege 'sanctum sanctorum',
Bombard your portals in my raids
    Upon lust's open forum,

And firing broadsides, salvos, shells,
    I'll Cortez your Peru,
And reach the Promised Garden's dells
    Where Adam's apple grew.

Harmonic unison we'll gain
    And pontracuntal bliss,
We'll cross our rhythms with our pain
    Till bar lines stave us, sis.

But I deceive myself, no doubt,
    You're certain to be ice-bound,
No pleasure from this glacial rout
    Shall I derive, but love's wound.

From bed to bed you've hopped, in troth,
    My Californian frill,
Too many jerks have spoiled your froth
    And basked upon your grill.

For I have come from Sweden's shores,
    Where blondes are tall and phallic,
Where nearly all the broads are whores
    And morals are barbaric,

And there I wenched with dolls and molls
    And fed on lechery,
And there as here their love involves
    Sig Freud's necessity,

Which makes amours so cold and chill
    There is no satisfaction,
Refrigerates a raptured thrill
    And freezes lovers' friction.

So I to London shall return
    To find Elysium
In Celia's arms which always burn
    My body till it's numb.

In England's isle the lasses live
    Whom you would think were prudes,
But when between the sheets they dive
    No dish is better stewed.

ROLAND MATHIAS

Fool's Fingers

Not everything is named, either
For memory's sake or the marks
In the book. And what's most secret,
Ridiculous in its fashion, has
Often no more of date than
Repeated omens, settings of twigs
Or stones, threatening the week
With another dervish appearance.

There had been snow that the noon
Sun melted. The sloping fields
Still had a snow-rash, the roughest
Grass clumps sparkily topped with white.
The nameless runnel that lower down
Brings a stick or two to Soar's
Unheeding backs like a wet bitch
Shaking herself dropped here
Suddenly through a culvert from left
To right of the road. The walled-in roar
It was pulled me, from habit, to peer
Down at the wintered split channel
And there, all but surfing the small
Blurt of water, hung a line of daredevil
Ice-shapes, onions, pears, inverted cold
Parsnips of ice that the bank's
Promiscuous trickles had dripped faster
Than one frost's icicles. Down
To the very tips they had run
To freeze, these water-joints, these
Drips without knuckles, pompously fived
And bladdered to make fool's fingers —
Not Struwwelpeter's with trumpery nails
But fat shilling digits with the heart's
Cold water blue in the ends. Later

I saw them everywhere, under the field's
Cornice, solemnly hung from a tree-root
Close to the shock of free water
But never quite carried away.
                    I doubt
That the day will stand, but the image
Will, as my heart fidgets off, gloving
Fool's fingers with a different colour.

ROBERT MINHINNICK

Short Wave

I try to tune in, but Europe's blurred voice
Becomes stranger with the movement of the dial.

All stations seem to give a fragment of
Performance — Mozart disarmed by a fizzled
Prodigy; innumerable cliques of wordsmiths.

As the electric crackles I make believe
I am composing an avant-garde symphony,
A sound poem for a hall of idiot speech.

But behind the static are moments of sanity:
A string quartet and interesting chanteuse;
Then histrionics at a play's climax.

For some reason, a hubbub of languages
And dim music becomes more important
Than any scheduled programme. It suits

My mood perhaps, this indecipherable mayhem
Of newscasters and sopranos, and the long
Returns to electronic gibbering.

Somewhere, behind a rock band's sudden squall,
A morse message is tapped out. For a few seconds
It is clear, articulate, before melting

Into Europe's verbiage. It was not mayday.
And I twist the dial a hairsbreadth into jazz.

GWLADYS E. LEWIS

Remembering Alun Lewis

Pengarreg, July 1st, 1974. It is Alun's birthday: the thirtieth I
have remembered in our own special way since his death in 1944.

Strawberries used to be cheap and plentiful on July 1st, so we,
as a family, celebrated Alun's birthday by a tea of unlimited
strawberries and cream. We called it a 'strawberry fuddle'. When
he died we decided that instead of mourning him on his death-
day, March 5th, we would give thanks for the joy and richness he
brought into our lives by his rare companionship on his birthday;
and that each member of the family, wherever he or she might be,
would, if humanly possible, have strawberries for tea, in happy
memory.

So now as twilight descends, having gone through the strawberry ritual, I allow myself a period of remembering . . .

It is Autumn 1915, Alun is a few months old, asleep in his cot
in the bedroom just above the living-room where my husband
and I are busy in our separate ways. A whimper from the
bedroom soon becomes a full cry and I fly upstairs. Gently I take
Alun's tiny hand in mine and whisper, "It's all right, darling,
mother's here" and immediately the cry sinks to a whimper, then
ceases. Soon Alun is asleep again. As I enter the living-room my
husband smiles and says, "Tell me, what magic do you use?" and
he shakes his head in masculine mystification.

The first world war is nearly over and my husband has been
wounded and discharged from the army with a badly shattered
knee. We have made the best house deal we can in these difficult

days and are starting to set up home for the second time in six years. Alun is in the front bedroom (he is now five) which overlooks the street. He is surveying the scene from the window as the furniture is moved in. Later, at tea, he says, "There's a little girl across the way who is prettier than she should be" — one of those innocent childish sayings that suggests more than is apparent on the surface.

Alun is about nine. It is evening, he is sitting deep in an armchair reading a newspaper. He calls out, "Mother, what is a suffragette?" Having been a dedicated suffragette, this is right up my street; so I tell him how the majority in a male House of Commons did not think women were intelligent enough to understand about education, houses, the poor and so on, and so refused to give them the right to vote. His reply is short and to the point: "What cheek!" and he wriggles back into the chair with his paper.

Now I am returning with him from a journey we made to Cowbridge for him to sit an examination for a boarder scholarship. He is very dissatisfied with his work and insists on talking about the papers. In the General Information paper a question asked "Who, or what, was the Widow's mite?" "I knew that," he says; "I put down — 'A fatherless child'." I have to use all my control to keep a straight face and refrain from screaming with delight at the ingenuity of the answer. When the headmaster wrote offering a scholarship, he asked if we knew that Alun had perpetrated a first class "howler".

Once again I feel the pride and the tears at a school prize day when Alun's story 'The Dwarf's Story" which has appeared in the school magazine is mentioned as a literary event of the school year. His English master, a cousin of Helen Waddell, author of *Heloise and Abelard* and a translator of the classics, has sent the story for her appraisal. She writes a personal letter to Alun, encouraging and advising him. I remember she charged him to be sparing with adjectives and 'wear down' his prose till only the basic essentials remained. She likened this to a soldier tempering his sword to a fine and cutting edge.

Alun has been on one of his solitary walks on the mountain above Cwmaman and has been caught in a thunderstorm. He comes home soaked through but happy. "Look mother," he says, and he passes me a paper on which are written two or three short poems. One of them, 'Five Slender Birches' was published in *The Sunday Times* I think, and another, 'Nosegay' in which he made pretty play with the names of wild flowers was also published in one of the Sunday papers. But the first poem he ever had published was in the 'Wales day by day' column of the *Western Mail*. It was 'On the death of Queen Astrid', the beautiful wife of King Leopold of the Belgians who was killed when a car in which she was travelling and her husband driving went out of control and crashed into a tree in a Belgian forest. All Europe was shocked by the tragedy.

Remembering the thunderstorm brings me to an incident that occurred one summer when we were staying at the Mill Cottage in Penbryn and Alun was on holiday from Aberystwyth University. He had started back from Llangrannog after tea, walking along the coast to Penbryn, up cliffs and down to small coves all along the way. The light soon began to fade and to add to his difficulties a terrific thunderstorm broke over the coast. Thunder rolled and roared among the caves and coves and lightning flashed and struck. The rest of the family was safely in the Mill cottage but growing more and more worried over Alun. It was so dark that at times he had to wait for a lightning flash to see his way past a dangerous rock formation, and when he finally crossed the last cliff he still had to navigate the big, Penbryn beach and a steep rough path before he reached the cottage. We were discussing ways and means of organising a search party in an isolated rural area when the door opened and there in the lamplight stood Alun dripping wet from head to foot, completely exhausted physically, but exhilarated in spirit.

Now I am home again in Aberdare, where we have moved from Cwmaman, and I remember Alun telling me of an incident that happened at a local dance hall the night before. He was home from Aber and passed a hall where popular dancing was in progress. Being unaware of class, Alun went in for a while to enjoy one of his favourite pastimes. A pretty girl spotted him and took the initiative to ask him for more than one dance. The last was the last of the evening, and as it ended she kissed him full on the lips. I still feel amused when I think of the conflict he must have felt between his natural gallantry and his fastidious tastes.

115

I am beginning to feel tired as befits an old lady who has travelled in thought so far in time. So here is my final picture before I return to reality.

Alun is now married and has been doing me some kindness. I thank him for being such a good son, and he tells me it is far easier to be a good son than a good husband — to which sentiment I'm sure all true husbands will say 'Amen'. The mother-son relationship is a much simpler one than that of husband and wife. I remember my own dear husband telling me his highest ambition was to be a success as a husband, and in that he triumphed — gloriously.

As I close, I repeat to myself Alun's last message to me before he sailed to India:

Be *ye* also tranquil, especially, Gwladys Elizabeth.

To give a graceful finish I add a poem of Alun's that M. Gilbert of Paris sent to me some time ago. M. Gilbert was the librarian in the School of Peace in Pontigny. It was founded a year or two before the last war to try and avert the impending conflict. Alun spent six weeks in Pontigny in the summer of 1938 or 1939 as a representative British student. The poem refers to a special day Alun and M. Gilbert spent together and it is much in tune with my present mood —

> Day I have loved
> I close your eyes
> And fold
> Your dead white hands.

JOHN POWELL WARD

Here, Home

Then I got home, very late, and parked the
car, by the hedge, and entered the porch,
and was turning the key, when I heard a
single fox bark, a mile away, and I went
inside, put down my suitcase, and spread

my fingers on the wall to find the light-
switch, and one bulb lit dimly, and the
terrier, lying on the carpet, opened one
eye, after a second's pause, and then, a
little later, he seemed, gradually, to be
moving, and raising himself, on rear legs
only, and then the front, with an effort,
and then walked, extremely slowly, about five
steps, to me, where his nose stopped, barely
a quarter-inch, from my trouser-leg, where
he stood, in a kind of acknowledgement, as
it were, and my fingertips touched his wire
head, and I heard, a very tiny breathing, as
of two small people, perhaps, and at the top,
of the stairs, the bedroom door, half-opened,
yielded a cot, with a still form, what I
knew to be, tousled sheets, and one half of
a small, curly head of hair, exposed, like
an object I perceived, or was expert on,
and a little body, under the sheets, which
went up, and then back, so carefully, and
I walked, still with my overcoat on, along
the passage, past another bedroom, in which
a bigger boy slept, and a further door,
also, was open, to its bedroom, where a
wife lay, in black pyjamas, asleep, the
face loaded, very full, but pre-empted for
the night, and by her, in the double bed,
was a space, the shape and size of a man,
into which I climbed, fitting it, exactly,
and lay half-asleep, templating it, or would
seem so, to a further fox or man who arrived.

117

SEAMUS HEANEY

The Train

I used to lie with an ear to the line
For that way, they said, there should come a sound
Escaping ahead, an iron tune
Of flange and piston pitched along the ground.
But I never heard that. Always, instead,
Struck couplings and shuntings two miles away
Lifted over the woods. The head
Of a horse swirled back from the gate, a grey
Turnover of haunch and mane, and I'd look
Up to the cutting where she'd soon appear.
One field back, in the house, small ripples shook
Silently across our drinking water —
As they are shaking now across my heart —
And vanished into where they seemed to start.

BOBI JONES

Order, Purpose And Resurgence In Poetry

The most stimulating aspects of poetry are those that have always existed, and not the more ephemeral and superficial flotsam and jetsam of recent fashion. At the present time, with such obvious oppression by the 'new' and a brainwashing through advertising media to accept the 'latest' as ubiquitously the best, the unpopular quest for the permanent and evergreen in art has become a challenge for only the most tenacious spirits. The quest is even more of a challenge and an adventure in that it requires a recognition that the new is necessarily an inherent part of what is permanent and that to grasp the durable one can only move forward into a 'post-new' and not return to a pristine 'pre-new' condition of no change.

Searching out permanent roots tends to become a matter of necessity to the contemporary Welsh poet, as to be Welsh in the present crisis entails a unity in time as well as in place and compels each of us to utilise all the resources at our disposal in order to exist. The Editor has asked me for a personal response to the poetic predicament of our day, and I think that there are three points I can briefly name that stem from this consciousness of a contemporary exploration of the permanent.

During recent years such ideas as I have about literature have crystallised in three ways, and I have been trying to note them down in a trilogy of volumes, two of which have been completed — *Tafod y Llenor* (The Writer's Tongue) and *Diben y Llenor* (The Writer's End) — and the third of which is wearily under way, bearing currently the provisional title *Deunydd y Llenor* (The Writer's Material). One possible effort at solving the problem the Editor has set me would be to say something about what each of these volumes contains; but perhaps a brief personal preamble may explain some of the presuppositions that underline their different themes.

I was born into a non-Welsh-speaking family in the city of Cardiff, and the Welsh language took me over during adolescence. My natural habitat is, of course, cynical agnosticism; but a violent conversion well after reaching manhood got rid of all hopes I had of being anything but a broken and orthodox Calvinist for the rest of my days. The ironic literary environment of nihilistic absurdism sprinkled with surrealism and anti-poetry, and the usual European, South and North American 'names' of modernistic stereotypism, were my daily bread during my formative years; but my deepening interest in such matters as Guillaumian linguistics has led me to reorientate completely my attitude to the use of language, and this new sense of the 'intuitions of order' has been substantially reinforced by some studies in depth of the Welsh literary tradition. So I now find myself, much to my own consternation, sailing in a directly opposite direction to many of my colleagues and contemporaries in verse, short stories and literary criticism, not to mention linguistics and religion.

This may take some explaining.

Let me begin by touching on the last of the three points I made — the one regarding 'intuitions of order'.

Since the romantic period, literary critics have made a great deal of capital out of the intuitiveness necessary to the inspired, muse-ridden poet, and most of us (as long as it is modified with one or two genuflections in the direction of hard work and craftsmanship) would go along a fair part of the way with this high respect for the unseen seams of poetic power. Unfortunately, this due regard for intuitiveness got unseemingly tied up with the reaction against classical order, with Freudianism, and automatism, and made the unjustified supposition that the truly significant intuitions were necessarily unorganised and even disorganised.

I am now soundly convinced that this aberration was completely wrong and could only be a very temporary deviation in what has to be, by the very nature of things, the mainstream of creative literature. Just as language is utterly dependent on order, so literature (despite all protests to the contrary) gets its lifeblood from the same source. One finds the word 'form' bandied about pretty freely by Welsh critics; but too often when faced with the adult task of defining the essential nature of 'form', they slink back to impressionistic and subjectivist essay-writing and fluff the challenge of getting to grips with the deep things of language. Amongst the many discoveries made in the field of linguistics, Gustave Guillaume demonstrated that the truly crucial structures of language were inevitably shaped on the basis of and maintained by extra-linguistic intuitions of structures — for example, the simple and unmeditated contrast between absence and presence, and the inherent sense we have of *gravity* and its by-products 'dependence' and 'falling'. With a mass of detail, filling scores of volumes (a mere eight of which have hitherto been published) Guillaume went into fascinating detail about the way languages have dynamically patterned themselves — quite unconsciously of course, without obvious direction by any individual, — and are only able to exist because of this central core of unseen order. We think within these pre-determined channels.

Gustave Guillaume is not a well-known figure in English linguistic circles. Although a complete page was devoted recently to reviewing a posthumously published book of his in the T.L.S., on the whole English linguists seem now almost *en bloc* to be deeply entrenched American and Chomskyan in orientation. In France, on the other hand, where Meillet spoke of Guillaume as "un des esprits les plus distingués d'Europe", the first shock of Chomskyanism seems now thankfully to be fading and a realisation of what this other rather difficult but more brilliant genius was doing in their midst, seems during the last three years to be emerging.

My own conviction is that just as each language has two levels, as Saussure claimed, namely *langue* (the organising structures) and *parole* or *discours* (the external expressions), so too literature has come into being through a similar two-fold architecture, but one that has borrowed the materials already within language and adopted the same methods of structuring itself. Despite all Romantic attempts to reject form (and even language itself), the escape from the inherent order of language has been completely foiled, and literature too remains worked through and through by intuitions of order.

Having come to accept this fact, and even to rejoice in it, — and humility before the necessities of existence is not something a poet (nor anyone else) takes to easily — one returns (singing) to the Welsh tradition, which is a contemporary force, and gains immense satisfaction from searching its hidden secrets and innermost systems. The amazing organization of *cynghanedd* and the much-misunderstood *mesurau* of the poetic craft, together with 'Irish rhymes' (which were as much Welsh as Irish) and *proest* and the alternate accented non-accented rhymes lead any inquisitive soul to ask, not the comparatively uninteresting question 'how', but the truly vibrating question of the adventurer 'why'?

Such adventures in form, bringing the excitement of discovery along with the muscular empathy of symmetry, have led me to a devouring attitude towards the possibilities of digesting the Welsh tradition in a way that is appropriate to it and our times. Whereas anarchy is intentional, each national language and literature has its own coherent patterning, and we are fortunate in Wales that we have a compact community, responsible for a powerful literary language, that has constructed a major literary heritage. The challenge to the Welsh poet, at the end of the twentieth century, emerging out of the dark tunnel of nihilism and concrete-poetry, hermeticism and surrealism, is to return without returning to the great strengths that are available to him.

He can not be reactionary, in the twentieth-century sense; but unless he penetrates to the core of his own Welsh literary forms, he will probably be swept along willy-nilly by the drib-drab fashion-mongering non-poetry that lies in wait to ambush the unwary and unintelligent contemporary imitator.

My Calvinism, too, is no doubt unashamedly related in a profound way to this experimental insistence on order, and is central to that point as it is to the third matter I hope to discuss later on. Having come through adolescence slightly to the left of the communists, pacifist, and convinced that the supernatural was unconvincing, taking over the usual dogmas of my post-Hiroshima generation regarding the primitive myths of the New as well as the Old Testament, rejecting the Trinity (except in the usual acrobatic interpretative manner) and rejecting everything else I found inconvenient, I had a rude awakening, as the saying goes, in my maturity. A shattering interruption. And although its significance at the time was far from intelligible, I eventually found to my dismay that the only really adequate expression of what I now knew, was to be found — of all places — in the Calvinist interpretation of Christianity. Historical Christianity.

Calvinism is often dubbed 'systematic', which is for some one way of damning it, and of getting rid of a rather nasty problem. The label has a great deal of truth about it as long as one keeps in mind that we are here dealing with a volcanic system, fierce and 'foolish', numinous and knowledgeable. The flamboyance of Pantycelyn and the unwise vitality of Howell Harries as contrasted with the dull sobriety of the detached 'seeker', is what characterises the dynamic of this particular 'system'. Hills skipping and valleys clapping hands are more in keeping with such an exhilarating 'system' than the jaded restraint of agnostic despair.

Further discussion of that point here would be irrelevant. But it was essential for me to refer to this most basic experience in order to explain what my attitude has been to the philosophy of the absurd.

An inhering strand of the main Welsh literary tradition has been the continuing presence from the very beginning of an Augustinian-Calvinist ideology. No one who really grasps the inner character of our literature can escape from the penetrating consciousness of this great intellectual backbone. It has been a formative influence in the vitalising of our literature through multitudinous vicissitudes. The Calvinist's God-centred pre-suppositions are ever and always directly in opposition to the autonomous humanist's. The humanist, when he ventures so far as to claim any purpose to literature outside itself or himself (and of course, the usual line is to search within the confines of literature for its own *raison d'être*), predictably turns Marxist. The Marxist at least seems to have grasped the simple proposition that language can never be independent, always has to say something, and is by nature an analysis of the universe in which we live. The masturbating or self-indulgent critic of the West who claims that literature exists in and for itself seems to have failed to get off the ground language-wise, and is trying to erect an unconvincing ivory tower between man and common sense.

The dogma of autonomous literature is related to the dogma of autonomous man. And while man is agonizingly conscious and only conscious of his own mortality, and while he remains for himself the unique centre of things, it is inevitable that the senselessness of his own existence should not only move him religiously but should be adopted into his philosophy of literature. If there is no purpose to his being, then there is no point to his literature either.

Now I am not here going to try to outline the usual well known arguments in favour of absurdism in order to shoot them down, as the whole position has long seemed to be patently absurd. But it is my own conviction that literature has always and will always gain its real *raison d'être*, even though men may choose to deny it, from outside itself. Its very existence as literature, the simple act of writing, is of course a denial of absurdism; and non-writing — out and out silence — is the only effective way of incorporating the sincere absurd experience in 'literary' form.

Having been brainwashed from childhood, like everyone else, in the contemporary secular mind, taking for granted the obviousness of secular attitudes to art, education, language, politics and so on, it proved difficult for me to reconstruct for myself from the very foundations as it were, a completely opposite philosophy, though I found a great deal of help in developing a classical Christian standpoint on all matters from a remarkable group of thinkers centred on Amsterdam, people like Herman Dooyweerd, H.R. Rookmaaker, and G.C. Berkouwer, and Dutch *émigrés* to the States such as Cornelius Van Til. The Welsh tradition of praise, so succinctly described in the note-books of the bardic schools, took on itself a more intelligible dimension when seen within this Augustinian-Calvinist context.

So, a second challenge I see emerging and being articulated for the Welsh poet at the end of the twentieth centure — cheek by jowl with his call to order and the intuitions of order — is this passionate recapture of a sense of purpose.

Which leads me on to a third position.

As I am convinced that secular Welsh Nationalism will only gain health the less secular (and if I may say so, the less political) it is in its core, it would seem obvious to me that, although some of its adherents pretend to be upholders of literary autonomy, absurdism, and so on, the very fact of an ideology centred on a culture external to themselves and a social heritage beyond their own egoisms denies the coherence of their standpoint. For the moment, allow me to be narrowly personal.

I was born a Cardiffian. One of the revolutionary experiences of my life (a life somewhat pockmarked with revolution) was to move from an anglicised provincial background, with the usual colonial overtones, to a thoroughly Welsh (some say belligerently Welsh) milieu. The unfortunate belligerency is partly a reaction against a defensive attitude found amongst Welsh speakers (*Adfer* is a fair example) that leads some to ignore areas of Wales whence the language has partly retreated. For me, the Welsh language is a unifying factor, territorially, historically and psychologically and is as much the possession and responsibility of the Cardiff man as the man from Llŷn. Welshmen in general are called to a massive and impossibly heroic task. One of the main themes of my verse has been this thing that has happened to me in microcosm — namely the reconquering of lost land, together with replanting it physically and mentally. Remorse and resurrection.

In the fifties, when I began to take poetry seriously, the purposelessness of existence, by then the norm amongst intel-lectuals, had split over inevitably in the Welsh mind to the purposelessness of Wales itself. Subjects such as 'Difodiant'

(Annihilation) and 'Adfeilion' (Ruins) had become the staple diet of even the Eisteddfod. The energy of literary creation had waned for more than a decade and the national nerve had cracked not only politically and religiously but artistically. The inferiority proclaimed legally and structurally for the Welsh nation by its eternally established peripheral position in the universe, possessing no centre of gravity within itself, was symbolically crystallised in our national psychology by the situation of our defining and historical language.

A blow in the face of this acceptance and coercion was a blow in favour of creativity. A resurgence out of this national succumbing was also for me a positive act in favour of literary fruitfulness. Breaking free from the uniformity of anglicised, centralised existence was paralleled by a grasp of the combined unity and diversity of poetic form.

I cannot divorce Welsh revival from purposeful and ordered poetic survival, for the social act of resuscitating the national life of Wales coincides with the creative urge to crack the encrusted torpor of literary negativity and raise in its place the purging zest of praise.

This discovery of Wales also permitted the mind to bypass London and to discover the brotherhood of nations in similar predicaments — not only because of old colonialisms or even the more modern varieties, nor merely on an economic or political or linguistic level — but psychologically and therefore artistically. The principle of combining the unity of internationalism with the diversity of nationalism so necessary on the political plane was echoed by a similar combination in literature. Wherever so-called 'unity' became ascendant (and uniform), the fruitful variety of shape and content was flattened out; but wherever this so-called and seemingly opposing 'variety' was uncontrolled, then chaos and anarchy too were let loose.

Bypassing London and realising relationships with the Basques and Bretons, Quebeckers and Kurds, African liberating movements and Ukranians, Jews and Arabs, have not only brought about new and sobering literary connections and interests, but also forced one to appreciate England, the resplendent England (not the abstract 'variety') that still seems to survive and may emerge more interestingly as so-called Britain is redefined and

London felicitously declines in significance. Bypassing London may also save one from the fate I sometimes have nightmares about during long winter nights when I suddenly wake up and imagine that none of this had happened and that I was an Anglo-Welsh writer (and what is worse an Anglo-Welsh critic) whining about the dangers of introversion, parochialism and over-indulgence in *engagement* and proclaiming moronically that art is more important than nationhood, as if art existed on the moon, and that the acme of self-criticism means yawning at decadent non-conformity, and that Welsh irony is something to do with tee-total hymns and sexy druids on the top of a tip or nitwits in fields.

These three troublesome bees in my bonnet which I have tried inadequately to let loose on these pages — formal intuitions, purposeful praise, and linguistic revivalism — have each and all provided thematic material for such verse as I write. But for me, just as interesting, and perhaps more fundamental, has been the way they have also deepened my abiding appreciation of the inherent verse-patterns themselves.

JOHN DAVIES

How To Write Anglo-Welsh Poetry

It's not too late, I suppose . . .
You could sound a Last Post or two
and if you can get away with saying
what's been said, then do.

First, apologise for not being able
to speak Welsh. Go on: apologise.
Being Anglo-*any*thing is really tough;
any gaps you can fill with sighs.

And get some roots, juggle names like
Taliesin and ap Gwilym, weave
A Cymric web. It doesn't matter what
they wrote; look, let's not be naive.

Now you can go on about the past
being more real than the present —
you've read your early R.S. Thomas,
you know where Welsh Wales went.

Spray place-names around. Caernarfon.
Cwmtwrch. Have, perhaps, a Swansea
sun marooned in Glamorgan's troubled
skies; even the weather's Welsh, see.

But a mining town is best, of course,
for impact, and you'll know what to say
about Valley Characters, the heart's dust
and the rest. Read it all up anyway.

A quick reference to *cynghanedd*
always goes down well; girls are cariad;
myth is in; exile, defeat, hills . . .
almost anything Welsh and sad.

Style now. Nothing fancy: write
all your messages as prose then chop
them up — it's how deeply red and green
they bleed that counts. Right, stop.

That's it, you've finished for now —
just brush the poems down: dead, fluffed
things but your own almost. Get
them mounted in magazines. Or stuffed.

RUTH BIDGOOD

Safaddan

Through bruised reeds my boat thrust
into open water. First light broke thin mist
and was broken in a scatter of brightness
on the grey lake. In the depths
Llyfni coursed, eternally separate,
spurning the lake-waters beyond
intangible banks of its own force.
Silent lay the drowned city of legend
with its aqueous colonnades.

I had never seen the lake so thronged with birds
or known them so quiet. Hundreds there were,
out on the water, on the island,
and secret among the reeds.
On the further shore, three horsemen
rode to the lake's edge. Two dismounted,
each in turn shouting over the water —
I could not hear the words. From all
that intricate pattern of stilled wings
and watchful eyes, not one bird startled up.
The shouting sank dully into the lake.

Now the third rider, tall on a tall white horse,
slowly paced down to the hushing waters,
dismounted, knelt in prayer. I shipped my oars
and was quiet as the birds. When he stood
in the growing sunlight, knowledge came to me.
I knelt in the boat. He called.
All round me, suddenly, were wings
beating the water, rustling the reeds,
and a thousand songs of homage rose.
My boat rocked on the joyful surge
of Llyfni's invisible stream, my ears
were dazed with triumphant proclamations

of sunken bells, and louder and louder
the All Hails of Safaddan's birds.
Lake and kingly rider and host of birds,
and I with them, were caught up into the sun.

Fragmented sun on sliding water:
reed-beds thick at the lake's verge:
the island low astern. Three distant riders
dwindling on a path away from the shore.
Tired, I reached for the oars.
I had never seen so many birds
on the lake. They were lifting, one by one
or dense in wedge-shaped flights.
It was quiet. There was only
my oars' creak-and-plash
and the soft rush of departing wings.

JOHN POWELL WARD

Editorial

After a deliberately open-ended period it is perhaps useful to take stock.

Everybody knows the usual description of how we got where we are now. Prior to this century there was lttle Welsh poetry in English. The rise of universal secondary education in Wales, however, put Welsh people in touch first-hand with a wider culture, offering new educational opportunities both liberal and vocational. This however was bought at the price of the medium; the English, rather than Welsh, language. At first therefore the implicit new possibility of a truly Welsh poetry but in English was greeted by the linguistically indigenous with huge suspicion; and not at all unjustified, in that the response of many Welsh who would enter that wider culture was to head for the gateway city of London, commonly affecting also some identity with it if not stage-clowning a 'Welshness' for happy metropolitan consumption. With the emergence in the '30's of a rather more coherent group,

Oxbridge or (and?) U. of Wales educated in many cases, some culturally autonomous consciousness grew even with the 'Anglo' prefix; still not enough to allay hostility from the Cymry. In the 1960's a second group emerged, associated with the names of Meic Stephens, Harri Webb, Raymond Garlick, John Tripp, Roland Mathias, Ned Thomas, Anthony Conran and many others, intent on mounting an Anglo-Welsh poetry, but one this time aspiring to a Welsh poetry in English as something distinct from the English tradition itself, and thus national, or at least ethnic, and emphatically not the dreaded 'provincial'. They established a critical community and milieu, some assessment of poets already well-known, and the magazines and publishing apparatus for dissemination; they also put together an Anglo-Welsh poetry of very clear profile such that, if the debate with the Welsh-language arm has continued, it has been to answer questions about linguistic validity, not so much about betrayal. So much is the backcloth for the present situation, and if all this sounds like a history thesis let it be hastily pointed out, should any be unaware of it, that all the above-named people are alive, highly active, centrally influential and not senile.

Some might feel that this group displayed the signs character-istic of embattled bodies driven by conviction and attempting headway against odds: a certain internal morale-lifting tendency and the easily-identified ritual imagery. To risk doing them injustice, they were suspicious of 'experiment' and certainly any beat modishness — and its effect on England — and reluctant to give precious magazine space to possibly infectious outsiders. But they were also more aware of the dangers of banner-waving than that view suggests: of the "identikit Anglo-Welsh poem" as Harri Webb called it (his squibs and *mots* were and are the most quotable source from this group and its writings); of the need for an intellectual restraint and sense of qualification, as Roland Mathias' criticism epitomizes, and of the contrasting yet con-sistent need (still not met) for a satirical and impolite mode to balance the easy nostalgia of which they were often, not always fairly, accused. Only *Second Aeon* — and Harri Webb — did very much about that. There was also a vigorous debate on the poetry-country issue, and which must come first.

If someone wonders why one is elaborating all this, suggesting stock-taking is needed and picturing clapped-out relay-runners collapsing heroically in exhaustion as they hand on the torch, consider this: that of the thirty-five poets who appeared in the Winter '71 and Spring '72 issues of this magazine, only *three* appear in either the present number or the last ordinary issue, Winter 1977. Of course this is partly chance, and a number more have appeared recently and will be in future issues. But other, much wider, factors present themselves. This magazine, if one may for convenience centre on it, was founded by Meic Stephens in 1965; that is, before university expansion and the student revolution, before inflation, the decline of affluence and the end of automatic Tory rule, before the Vietnam withdrawal and its easy poetic target, before EEC membership, before Ireland's troubles became explicit, before sociology, before the women's movement, and before the long run-in to the crystallizing of what we all now call 'devolution'. The situation the Sixties group encountered does not exist and there are no easy summaries of what does. Some attempt must therefore be made, for with a certain lull in the air we shall otherwise quickly be talking about 'quiet progress', 'periods of consolidation' and other terms suitably constipative. Time's digestive system is doubtless cyclical but more than the occasional belch might be expected from the after-lunch stupor — for example the one on the HST from Newport to Reading, which technological miracle, in speed, silence and (Arts Council-sponsored) comfort, parallels exactly our period from a notional 1970 that has flashed past so amazingly imperceptibly. The period has quietly produced many good collections and much detached and thorough criticism; exactly what the earlier group worked for, in fact, but the time comes to delineate, not it, but its progeny.

The list of poets whose *first* appearance came in the last seven years includes Graham Allen, Tony Curtis, Sheenagh Pugh, Alan Perry, Robert Minhinnick, Steve Griffiths, Jon Dressel, Nigel Jenkins, Duncan Bush, Christine Furnival, and at least ten others who have published more than the sporadic poem on isolated occasions. (That list leaves out an in-between group of Gillian Clarke, Ruth Bidgood, Peter Finch and others, but they will know what we mean and perhaps not mind illustrating the

131

necessary limits of all such groupings in any case.) Most are young but not that young. They win Gregory Awards, get in the Arts Co (GB), PEN and Poetry Yearbook anthologies and on 'Poetry Now'. The continuum of their attitudes to poetry is probably wider than that found in the sixties but their debate is less public. In fact they do not state what areas, if any, should be debated; if they are nationalist it is less overt and perhaps even more taken for granted than previously; poetically, if not socially, they work apart. Few of these poets write articles or reviews. Most are products of the university expansion world. Most important, the subject of their poetry is nowhere near so homogenous as that of the earlier group. They may write about hitchhiking in Montana; setting up a life; about material gathered delving into ancient civilizations by no means always Celtic; the nuances of social distinctions as expressed by material ones; travel; incidents in mental homes and hospitals; and, to some extent, what can still inadequately only be called the pop scene. A few go a little more overtly for a Welsh setting, others are nearer to the urban world identified nowhere. It is a quiet voice, seeming to wait for whatever message may be read in any setting or relationship, micro or macroscopic. It is not non-committal but is never strident. Perhaps paradoxically, it is a poetry of home.

Their relationship with the Saesneg scene is equally unclear. The sometimes defensive but necessary and ultimately productive attitude of the earlier group to the English influence was part of the deeply-felt aim, at least as far as poetry is concerned, to make English a Welsh language once and for all. But since now, unlike before, even so far-sighted an observer as Patrick Moore himself could scarcely say what English poetry *is* there is correspondingly less likelihood of the provincialism and campfollowing to any unified outside lead the earlier poets were set against. Any danger that the (Anglo-Welsh) centre will not hold derives now not from some London-based conspiracy but from its plurality: chaos in Earls Court Square, the poetry-reading circus, the American dominance, Bob Cobbing and other noises, the David Jones following, 'commitment' at Newcastle and the Manchester-based return to strict measure and rhyme. University literature departments do not know what to teach, there

132

are ten thousand magazines and the poetry triple crown has been won by Ireland.

All that may sound cynical but need not be seen as such. (The present writer, not entirely impartially, sees a greening in poetry across the border though would be hard pressed to describe it.) What needs stressing is that, in Wales at least, the efforts made a decade or more ago resulted in the base and apparatus from which such tentative pluralizings in the Welsh-in-English scene can now stem. Formula: the confidence of identity enables cultural diversification. The previous establishment of a poetic unity is what now enables its development in many directions. In Marxist terms adapted; a poetic movement must be fulfilled in order to be abolished. Not that this new group is near to achieving such developments. As the latest wave of 'Welsh poetry in English' (if they so see themselves, which they may not) they have a long way to go. None, yet, compares with such as Leslie Norris or John Ormond, let alone the awesomely self-sufficient vicar of Aberdaron. There is plenty of time for one of them, or one who prefers anonymity, to build a distinctive body of poetry, precisely because the present period is not yet defined or formed.

What we may need, if it does not sound too sententious, is a certain trust that the sense of identity sought a decade back is now adequate, that those poetically born into it can assume its existence, and with sufficient assurance to take poetic risks knowing that that will add to and enrich, rather than weaken, any tradition of Welsh poetry in English that exists and to which the poet feels allegiance. If English does have a distinctly Welsh usage then we can create from it, and create it, as well as argue it into existence. Such a thing is never guaranteed, but something in which one puts one's faith of course never is. That surely is cultural maturation.

NIGEL JENKINS

Where Poems Came From

They came, I supposed, from London.
Or from somewhere in England — Heaven,
most likely: wasn't God, after all, a bit
chalky — the grey suit and silver hair,
the underwear somewhat neglectful —
wasn't he the sort, in his spare time,
   to be spinning out rhymes
   on the prettiness of things?

Journeys they claimed —
   over hills and vales,
   through moonlit doors,
   down the last furlong
   from Ghent to Aix —
    but they reached us
too heavy for words with chalk-dust.
They were chalk-dust and the tired eye,
they were trembling knees when all went
speechless at the eager end of Friday.
They were paper and they were
   words, books of them
yellowed in the classroom cupboard —
the place that poems truly came from.

Yet truly they came,
behind my back they talked
to me, though I heard no words,
their coming was not to do
with words.
   It was in the laughter of dogs
   way across the snow. I could smell it
   in freshly painted rooms, taste it warmer
   in the cream than the milk. In the tricks
   that skies played with stone I found it,

I found it in my body when first
I discovered its emptying joy
and wanted, afraid, to share it.

They came too in forgotten
things, in the thing wholly strange —
     that I recognized.
And one mart-day they came,
in a farmer's voice as he sat
drinking tea,
    explaining to himself, trying
    to explain the world to himself.

But not in the words of his explanations,
not from the names did they come.
    For there's a space
    in things, a gap between
    the words for it and a wave's
    movement, its infinite motion.
As I stood,
    a baby, at the sea's edge
    I began to wail — for no misery
    no joy that I could name —
    lost, quite lost for words

to be facing there our world's great noise,
    to be facing there its silence.

DANNIE ABSE

Imitations

In this house, in this afternoon room,
my son and I. The other side of glass
snowflakes whitewash the shed roof and the grass
this surprised April. My son is 16,
an approximate man. He is my chameleon,
my soft diamond, my deciduous evergreen.

135

Eyes half closed, he listens to pop forgeries
of music — how hard it is to know — and perhaps
dreams of some school Juliet I don't know.
Meanwhile, beyond the bending window,
gusting suddenly, despite a sky half blue,
a blur of white blossom, whiter snow.

And I stare, oh immortal springtime, till
I'm elsewhere and the age my cool son is,
my father alive again (I, his duplicate)
his high breath, my low breath, sticking to the glass
while two white butterflies stumble, held each
to each, as if by elastic, and pass.

NIGEL WELLS

Y Plygaint

In the season of Winter
The final and first
Small skin covered god
Breathed to life

In dire of the weather
Our hope into bone
We wake at his waking
To light

The faithful report
Troop to the several sites

You Cardigan ladies
On with the lace
French chalked to heighten the white

We travel by candelling
File behind flare
Pilgrim in tallow fired night

Chapel and church call their scatter
The faithful repair
Luminous choirs in a gather
Carollers lit in the rare

Oh Lord hear our seasonal singing
Our tunefully outfitted air
Our stream of particular worship
Small Lordly in snowing
Our prayer

Bells make silver of drear
Cut it to clear
Ring and rouse by their ringing
The pious to praise

Sound of them strays
Steel peelers reeling the phrase
Dinning the ear lest the sensory's veer
Iron on the brassy cast plays

The joyfully word

Our Lord under litter
In draperies curled

Love's little lad in the world

He here
The gloria gongs

Sharpened to man shape
Great God's little snip
We make our oblation in writ

We thin on the ground
Would be throng on the air
And offer such verse as we dare

In season of winter these scribble and bits
Small saviour come down and the dove

Oh Lord in the greeny
Our Lord in the pink
We offer such jots
As we have

PHILIP OWENS

Grave

So here it is, where the worms wait.
Hell's letterbox? Poste restante
for all those resurrection hopes?

Gate of death and bed of hope
God says: joker, as always
toying with metaphors

    And so I.

It is his mouth of course, fixed
infinite grin.

RAYMOND WILLIAMS

Excerpt From An Interview

*Q. Can we now make the question of 'nation' quite different perhaps,
and more personal? A lot of your writing, even in clearly critical or
theoretical passages, is noticeably autobiographical. Has this any connection with Wales? What do you personally feel about this country?*

R.W. It's always rather puzzled me! You must remember I was
born on the border, and we talked about 'the English' who were

not us, and also 'the Welsh' who were not us. Actually if you look at it historically, our region as far back as you can trace — sixth century or so — was always some ambiguous state, you know, Erging or Ewyas and so on, little Welsh-speaking kingdoms being absorbed from one direction or another. But then I found to my surprise that many things I had thought were rather local to that border area, which was now anglicized Wales, were really only problems that existed in much of the rest of Wales, once I really started to talk to people who had come from other parts. And particularly this transforming experience of industrial South Wales, but also in the general tensions about the language in so much of the rest of Wales. So I was interested, but if I was asked where I was from, I would be rather precise about that area, that particular border area. I have got more and more interested because the ways in which what I think is the genuine Welsh revival have been going are ways which are very congenial to me. When it was Wales as simply another nationality, — well, you know it seems to me that the mix-up in these islands has been so great that this soon becomes a kind of myth-making, and I was tired of endlessly meeting a certain kind of very upper-middle-class Englishman (and there was nothing else you could call him) who would disclose at some point that he was really a Highlander or an Ulsterman or a Manxman, and it was clear he was nothing of the kind. Well, I didn't want to identify myself like that. And also some of the early phases of Welsh nationalism, I mean when we were the last bit of Christian Europe against the democratic and industrial tide and so on; it's powerful when anyone feels it, but there again Wales would be a very odd specimen in that one would have to abolish so much of the actual Wales for it to be plausibly that. But then when people started saying there are *specific* experiences of democratic communities, specific moral concerns within the religious tradition, specific attachments through language and the literature to values which are under pressure nearer the centre; and that out of this there are the materials for an alternative direction — all that positive emphasis, as well as the understandable but more negative emphasis that this is a neglected country (which I felt, because after all the area I came from was being depopulated through every generation of my family I can trace back, and I could see in my own family that

139

this was still happening) — when these feelings came together to identify themselves with Wales, I began to feel I could relate, and not just to my own area but to an entity one was then calling Wales. Although I still find it problematic; and whenever I have a really satisfactory conversation it is always when people raise these questions in the same way. Because I then find we're exploring reality rather than asserting a version of it which may be protecting us against it.

Q. Can one talk of an Anglo-Welsh poetry, as opposed to Welsh poetry or on the other hand a kind of regional poetry, or is this just an invention?

R.W. I wish I knew more about this; I see it asserted that the Welsh poet writing in English is doing something different from the English poet, and I can see in an amateur way some of this. Whether this is in his craft or in a set of feelings and references is often difficult to separate. I remember the ferocity of the attack of the Movement poets of the '50's on Dylan Thomas, as against that drunken, lurching, word-gas poetry, you know, and what was being pushed in its place was this certainly quite attractive verse of its kind, light social verse — a sort of shrug, polite, carefully not going beyond the emotions of what was probable, in almost a conversational prose which occasionally just to shape itself lurched into a kind of resonance. And they had ruled out the emotional intensity and the kind of writing that goes with it. I remember being very hostile, and it's the only time in my life since about 12 or 13 that I sat down after reading it and wrote in their manner, a poem called 'On First Looking Into *New Lines*' which was a piece of doggerel! Picking up from remarks like "a neutral tone is nowadays preferred" and this sense of limitation. I mean it seemed to me then that Dylan Thomas was not just another English poet.

Q. Is there something of an English-Welsh comparison there in the sense we mentioned earlier? Do writers like Pinter, for instance, use the language as a kind of voice only, with a lot of the words as 'solid objects' taken out, whereas with Dylan Thomas the word as a little gold nugget is being used all the time? I wonder what you think of R.S. Thomas' poetry for example, with its very material and natural references in single words.

R.W. Of course I respond very stongly to R.S. Thomas' poems because they are so very much of the same landscape, although a very different part of Wales, and this materiality of the country and the words is actually very difficult to separate in that kind of writing. And I don't feel that it's regional either, because 'regional' as a description suggests that the predominant characteristics are still national but with some slight local variation — I don't think this is slight. But it's difficult to trace out because I find that some northern poets for example are radically different from some southern English. I think the whole problem is not whether one can feel Welsh, although God knows that has problems enough, but I think that's a relatively simple thing next to the problems the English have about feeling English, because of the different parts of England, the real difference between the West country and East Anglia for example — and it seems to me huge — and the constant sense of difference I get from the North, especially since one has only the one term 'England' to describe all this. And given the *dominant* mode in this century in England, which has been very much South-East England, and a limited social part of that, then Wales is very sharply distinct, not in a regional way but in a way that is better called national.

Q. Doesn't one notice that the leading English poets of the time, Bunting, Larkin, Ted Hughes, Hill, are not from South-East England, in contrast to most Movement poets?

R.W. I do think that is an uncreative culture, of the South-East, that very effective administrative urban culture of the South-East; I mean I think they can do most things *except* these central matters of thinking and creating; although of course they control the conditions in which almost everybody else has to do them.

Q. You make the distinction in The Country and the City, *between not so much urban and rural but "forms of settlement" and "forms of exploitation". Is a small nation a form of settlement in that sense?*

R.W. I think it is, and I think it can become so. What I enjoyed as a change of generation in nationalism, for instance, was when people started talking about "this Wales we're going to make".

The feeling I have now, although sharing all the difficulties which I suppose every European shares, is that there is *actually* more of a sense, despite all the disagreements, of a future here, than there is in the parts of England where I work. For instance the South-East, which has this incredibly narrow and selective way of living, this turn-over on hire purchase, and that was all you really had in common. Now the jolt that got, from 1973 and the depression then, and the further jolt it's going to have when it is realised that that isn't temporary, — I think it really disorientated people, because at that point, theoretically anyway, socialism takes over, and yet there was no movement that way at all; none. People aren't reacting towards socialism from this crisis.

Q. Should they?

R.W. I think socialism has lost so much of its meaning, within the various political adaptations and suppressions that have gone on, that it has the problem of finding some positive content that people could identify with, and I think that that is only likely to happen if you've got something more than a critique of capitalism. You've got to have some sense of what genuinely would be a different way to live, because it would be hard enough to get; and if you've got merely a name, or the repetition of various heroic events elsewhere, then people will try to put something together which is visibly breaking to pieces, and this is very frustrating. You've got to have something much stronger and more positive if you're going to have a socialist movement which is a popular socialist movement.

Q. In The Country and the City *you warn against the danger of looking back for a communal, rural England that once was, finding that each century saw that in the one before, not in itself. Yet you say very little there about the earlier Celtic societies which some people in Wales in a sense look back to. The suggestion may not be that these should be revived, but certainly that they have been overlaid by the industrial and capitalist culture, whereas perhaps they could be rediscovered in some way as a basis to build on. Is this possible?*

R.W. I think it's the right question to ask, and this is something I'm now working on although I've never had much occasion to talk about it. I have become very preoccupied by the prehistory and early history of this part of the world, particularly in my own specific part. And the problem about it is that I find I'm thinking not only of the Celtic past but the pre-Celtic past, and I find I'm having to do this in very physical ways because of all the physical problems about a Celtic and pre-Celtic population. I've been spending my time this summer going round the relevant places which are very thick in the area where I grew up, precisely on the border between the Celtic and pre-Celtic populations, and I find that the history of that stage is very curious. Now I find when I do this that I'm not sure which *is* this 'past' that could be recovered. If I think of the radical, egalitarian, rural Wales, I think that is a creation of a long experience of domination and neglect, quite late, and I'm not sure it is much like the Celtic society which preceded it. Indeed I'm not sure about the relations between the Celtic society and the one it overlaid in Wales. So I think that what you can have very strongly in Wales because there's the great continuity of the language and the awareness of the difference in the past, is just the sense, which I think is very important at this stage in the twentieth century, that it is possible to *be* a different people. There isn't just one model. But I have a strong sense also that it will be much more made than recovered. Much harder than making the institutions that are required is having the feelings that make the institutions work, and I think there is a very rich resource for that in Wales. And I think that when I look at the literature — slowly learning to read it in Welsh, as well as English writing from Wales — I see something of this, although again not all, because an important part of early Welsh literature comes from a very different and very hierarchical society quite understandably, and is a very different kind of world.

Q. On a different point: all through from Culture and Society *and* The Long Revolution *to* The Country and the City *you have an emphasis on a social totality, a shared, collaborative culture, and this comes over in a very sane and indeed 'English pragmatist' way. You seem not to need a dimension of the mysterious or unknown, perhaps religious. What do you say to that?*

R.W. Well, it surprises me you put it that way although I think it could be perfectly fair. I must say that the things which have most surprised my own contemporaries, although it's been different with the younger generation, but certainly 'surprised' would be a mild word for my elders — is that I have said things that seemed to me the simplest common-sense, but which have been taken as this very odd way of thinking about society. And I have since been told, by people more thoroughly Welsh than I am, that I took this way of thinking with me out of rural Wales, however anglicized. I am not sure it is entirely that. On the point of other dimensions, of course the whole international socialist and Marxist movement is crucial, and in a sense I feel very European that way. I feel as close now to people battling it out at the edges, at the Left edges of the Italian communist party, I feel much more involved now in what they're doing than I do in English politics and that is crucial. But in the other thing you mention — I do in fact now have an attitude to land, to physical land, which is in one way very material, because what always interests me is how it was made. I have a very strong sense of people making landscape, and this is even after growing up in an area in which an important part is clearly not man-made although man-affected. And I do find that when I think about this, tracing these old hollow roads for example or looking at old barrows or even simply old fields, it feels like an experience or interest that other people call mystical or religious. It doesn't feel like common-sense although at another level I feel it is the most immediate common-sense. I know what happens when you cut a ditch, and I know the really extraordinary thing which still absolutely amazes me, that a man cutting a ditch four thousand years ago — his mark is still there; and I've seen it described, when it appears in other people's thinking, as a religious feeling. But it is a very strong feeling, that's all I can say.

Q. Is that kind of feeling at the centre of poetry, in the way that a social concern might be at the heart of many novels?

R.W. I think it's an incredibly important experience to express. I don't say it is impossible in a novel, in fact I'm going to attempt it. But with poetry, yes; I find a very strong tradition of writing which has that sense. This is the sense in which Hardy for instance is very important to me, and Clare and so on, and much modern Welsh writing is of great interest to me for that reason, the strong sense of the land.

Q. When one is cutting a ditch or reading a compelling poem, is the experience, if not timeless, certainly at a different dimension from social concern, so that that withers away? Not the actual suffering of people, but the arrangements, the social structures — do they fade away in the presence of this very direct, compelling experience?

R.W. I think it's a matter of attention. I think that if at the moment of attention one is having to say that other things don't matter, then the attention hasn't succeeded. There are moments when the attention is so intense, the writing or physical activity, that the other is not there; however this is different from negating it. Because if you negate it — and this is the system that some people have moved into — if you put this over *against* social concern, so that you have to choose between the two, then I'm not with that. But there are moments of attention which are absolutely crucial, and moreover I think the awareness of those ought to inform any social concern which is going to be good and human. Because otherwise social concern can become a very frustrating and shallow based thing. But I find I move from such moments of attention to thinking inevitably about the social order in this quite different sense, that out of something as absorbing and practical and obvious as it often is, as digging the ditch, building the wall, clearing the field — that out of such things the social order actually happens. And this is the interest of Marxism, which at its best is the one social philosophy that insists on this. It *is* from digging ditches and building walls, and not from kings and constitutions and so on, that history happens. And so I find you can move from these moments which for the time being are so important that only they are there, to this kind of thinking about the social order which can then go all the way. But if you start from the abstractions — and I notice this so much now about politics — it's not only that that's thinner than this other kind of attention, but that in the end it can't deal with what it's supposed to deal with.

Q. A final question. Should poetry, if it's not economically viable, be subsidized?

R.W. I have no doubt that it should be; and we have to call it 'subsidized' because that's the only term we can put to the sort of institutions that are going to give it. I've always taken a very simple view on this, that literature like all the other arts more than pays for itself, but it has a very complicated system of collecting its dues . . . If you look at any art in the world over sufficient time it has more than paid for itself in quite simple financial terms, not just that it has created other kinds of wealth. And really all a body giving money to a contemporary writer or magazine or company is doing, is arranging some credit, or realizing some already created value which it is advancing, so that this kind of work can continue. I don't regard it as taking money from something else to do this. I'm glad there is the pressure for this, and it's as crucial as that.

ALAN LLWYD

Excerpt From:*Cynghanedd* And English Poetry

Wilfred Owen died at the age of 25 in the First World War, and he died a major poet. Not only have his war poems never been rivalled for sheer terseness, tension and, to use his own word, compassion, but he was also a great technical innovator. Many poets and critics have completely disregarded these innovations as being a Welsh influence on his work. Cecil Day Lewis, for example, in his introduction to *The Collected Poems of Wilfred Owen* (Chatto and Windus, 1963), says that:

> Owen was not a technical innovator except in one respect — his consistent use of consonantal end-rhymes (grained/ground; tall/ toil). Consonantal rhyme, and other forms of assonance, are common in Welsh poetry and had been used previously in

146

English by Vaughan, Emily Dickinson and Hopkins. There is
no evidence that Owen had read any of the three last; nor could
he read Welsh — his parents were both English and he was born
in England.

Day Lewis concludes by saying, referring to the so-called consonantal rhyme in his work, that:

> Owen may well have discovered it for himself: a young poet's
> head is full of chiming sounds: it is a matter of nerve and skill,
> not necessarily of outside authority, whether he comes to use,
> deliberately and successfully, chimes which to orthodox ears
> would sound discordant.

I think that Cecil Day Lewis is rather misled about all this. Owen
has definitely been influenced by *cynghanedd* and Welsh prosody
in more ways than one. Of this I have no doubt whatsoever,
although I have never come across any real or concrete evidence
to back up my claim. The little evidence or possibilities I have I
will soon draw attention to, but there is no real need for that, as
the examples of *cynghanedd* and Welsh prosodic devices in
Owen's work really speak for themselves. Let us therefore discuss
these devices first of all.

Day Lewis mentions consonantal rhyme. This is, in fact, what
the Welsh term as *proest*, a sort of half-rhyme, which has already
been drawn attention to in connection with Hopkins. Many of
Wilfred Owen's poems have been written in this manner. Let us
take an example:

> "My Love!" one moaned. Love-languid seemed his *mood*,
> Till, slowly lowered, his whole face kissed the *mud*.
> > And the Bayonets' long teeth *grinned;*
> > Rabbles of Shells hooted and *groaned;*

Comparing the above lines to end-rhymes in the *englyn proest* by
Tudur Aled would soon show the resemblance between them:

> Bu adladd nowradd o'n *nerth,*
> Bu ddŵr Noe yn boddi'r *North;*
> Ba ryw sŵn — ai'r wybr a *syrth?*
> Bu ddiasbad heb *ddosbarth.*

Let us now look at some of his polysyllabic end-rhymes:

> Our brains ache, in the merciless iced east winds that *knive*
> *us* . . .
> Wearied we keep awake because the night is *silent* . . .
> Low, drooping flares confuse our memory of the *salient* . . .
> Worried by silence, sentries whisper, curious, *nervous,*
>
> Pale flakes with fingering stealth come feeling for our *faces* —
> We cringe in holes, back on forgotten dreams, and stare, snow-
> dazed,
> Deep into grassier ditches. So we drowse, sun-dozed,
> Littered with blossoms trickling where the blackbird *fusses.*

And again from another poem:

> I have been *witness*
>   Of a Strange *sweetness,*
> All fancy *surpassing*
>   Past all *supposing.*

These once again resemble Welsh *proest* rhymes, although the above examples are not really *proest* rhymes, but rather rhymes based upon *cynghanedd.* Here is another *englyn proest* by Tudur Aled with similar end-rhymes:

> Dewis byrth, nid oes *borthor,*
> Dewis barth y'n dwys *borthir;*
> Dewis borthiant *dosbarthwr,*
> Dosbarthus, dis *aberthwyr.*

Neither should one overlook the *cynghanedd* in

> snow-dázed : sun-dózed
> sn   d z d s n d z d

in the second stanza quoted above. Wilfred Owen has many poems which have *proest* end-rhymes, such as 'Futility', 'A Terre', 'The Last Laugh', 'The Show', 'Exposure', as well as the famous 'Strange Meeting'.

But Owen's preoccupation with Welsh prosodic devices did not end with *proest* rhymes. He also experimented with internal rhyme and with the elements of *cynghanedd Lusg*. Take, for instance, the following poem:

ELEGY IN APRIL AND SEPTEMBER
(jabbered among the trees)

Hush, thrush!
Hush, *missen-thrush, I listen* . . .
I heard the *flush* of footsteps through the loose leaves,
And a low whistle by the water's brim.

Be *still, daffodil!*
And *wave* me not so *bravely.*
Your gay gold lily daunts me and deceives,
Who follow gleams more golden and more slim.

Look, brook!
O run and *look,* O run!
The vain reeds *shook* . . . Yet search till gray sea heaves,
And I will find wind among these fields for him.

Gaze, daisy!
Stare up through *haze* and glare,
And mark the hazardous stars all dawns and eves,
For my eye withers, and his star wanes dim.

All the internal rhymes are in italics. It also has two lines based upon the principle of *cynghanedd Lusg*, which are:

And *wave* me not so *bravely.*

Gaze, daisy!

We also have here alliterative effects: "loose leaves . . . low"; "dawns and eves"; "star wanes dim" (s before t softens the t and produces a d sound in the rules of *cynghanedd*.)

Are there any other examples of *cynghanedd* in Owen's work? Indeed there are, and strangely enough his favourite *cynghanedd* seems to be the *Sain anghytbwys ddyrchafedig,* Hopkins' favourite. Here are a few examples by Wilfred Owen:

> A barge round old *Cérisy slowly slewed*

> *Vividly gloomy,* with bright darkling *glows*

> Bugles sang, *saddening* the *evening air*

> The *shadow* of the *morrow* weighed on *men*

> Bees *fumbling* and *fuming* over sainfoin-*fields*

> *Braiding*
> Of *floating flames* across the mountain brow.

A line such as:

> Clouding, half gleam, half glower,

seems to be hinting at *cynghanedd Sain* also, but is not correct. Owen also has strong alliteration in his verse which may be based upon the principles of *cynghanedd Groes* and *Traws,* for example:

> High *burning* through the outer *bourne*

or

> Passing the rays
> Of the rubies of morning,
> Or the soft rise
> Of *the moon;* or *the meaning*

or

> Red lips are not so red
> As the *stained stones* kissed by the English dead.

And the following stanza from 'Has Your Soul Sipped?' seems to prove beyond any doubt that Owen had a working knowledge of cynghanedd:

> Sweeter than *nocturnes*
>   Of the wild nightingale
> Or than love's *nectar*
>   After life's gall.

"Nightingale" and "gall" are *proest* rhymes. But notice the other rhymes — "nocturnes" and "nectar". They are not really rhymes; neither are they *proest*. What we have here is a *cynghanedd:*

> nóctŭrnes : néctăr
> n ct n   ct

based upon the principle of *cynghanedd Groes gythwys ddiacen.*

Having established the fact that Owen had access to Welsh *cynghanedd,* and that his poetry has many examples of various Welsh prosodic devices, we are then tempted to ask where he got it from. Let us first challenge a few assertions made by Cecil Day Lewis. Lewis says that there is no evidence that Owen had read Henry Vaughan or Emily Dickinson, who also experimented with half-rhyme, or Hopkins. True, but, as Jon Stallworthy's biography of Owen shows, Owen had many anthologies of poetry in his own personal library. He could have read Vaughan or Dickinson, although it is more than probable that he never read any Hopkins, since Hopkins' poems were not published in book form until 1918. But I don't think this really matters. I believe that Owen had a much more direct access to Welsh prosody than through the works of other poets. Cecil Day Lewis also claims that Owen could not read Welsh and that "his parents were both English and he was born in England". True, once again, but I think that Lewis oversimplifies matters. Owen was of Welsh ancestry, and he was born in the border town of Oswestry, which had many Welsh-speakers then, as it still has today. Stallworthy says this of the Welsh connection in *Wilfred Owen: a biography* (Oxford University Press and Chatto and Windus, 1974):

> The Owen family tree has its tap-root in Wales. Wilfred inherited from his father the legend that they were descended from Baron Lewis Owen who, during the reign of Henry VIII,

was Sheriff of Merionethshire. The truth of this tradition, passed down through generations of yeomen stock, can never be established. All that is known is that the line crossed the border into England sometime before Queen Victoria's accession to the throne.

It is true that Owen was not a fluent Welsh-speaker, but the Owen family was very conscious of its connection with Wales. In 1905, for example, at the age of 12, Wilfred Owen stayed with the Paton family at Glan Clwyd, Rhewl, and Owen writes to his mother saying: "I can count up to 10 in Welsh, & have learnt a few expressions".

But this, of course, is not enough. I think that maybe a chance meeting with a Welsh poet or *englynwr* in later years could have given Owen access to Welsh prosody, or may be an old book of verse in Welsh belonging to the family. It is important to remember that these things are not necessarily recorded. There is another possibility, but it is a very slight one: Owen had a copy of George Borrow's *Wild Wales* in his library, as Jon Stallworthy's biography shows, and Borrow alludes more than once to Welsh prosody in *Wild Wales*, although he never explains what *cynghanedd* really is. But he quotes couplets and *englynion* in *Wild Wales*, such as this couplet, mis-quoted as it is by Borrow:

> Av i dir Môn, cr dwr Menai,
> Tros y traeth, ond aros trai.

Or this *englyn:*

> Codais, ymolchais yn Môn, cyn naw awr
> Ciniewa'n Nghaer Lleon,
> Pryd gosber yn y Werddon,
> Prydnawn wrth dan mawn yn Môn.

Could a young poet like Owen have picked out the *cynghanedd* in such passages, with the little knowledge of Welsh that he had? I think this is more than possible.

NIGEL JENKINS

Shirts

She hangs out his shirts,
pins them by the tails
to the singing line.

She hangs out his shirts,
and in the pure green
that the lawn paints them
she can see her face:
I am his wife.

In the attention
of cushions, the soft
elisions of a door —
a voice, her voice
comes back to her:
he is my husband,
I am his wife.

I am the place
he returns to, his
hunger's home.
I build every day
a houseful of rooms,
of walls to enfold
the things that he loves.

She hangs out his shirts,
and the air they breathe
fills them with flight:
his gentle arms rage
flailing at the sky,
scratching and clawing
to catch up with the wind.

She hangs out his shirts:
he is her husband,
she is his wife.

BARBARA HARDY

Women Poets

"Poète, prends ton luth et me donne un baiser"
(*La Nuit de Mai* — Alfred de Musset).

Women poets have no Muses, because they are Muses. The role of the Muse varies a little from man to man, and from time to time, but it combines the support and inspiration of mother, mistress, wife, and secretary. If you play the T.S. Eliot game, and make imaginative wholes out of his box of heterogeneous events like being in love, reading Spinoza, the sound of the typewriter and the smell of cooking, you could write a poem called 'His Muse', in which the poet is reading Spinoza, or Spinozistically relaxing, while the Muse types his poem, having lovingly cooked the meal which sends out fragrant odours from the kitchen. Women of nearly all classes have been hampered, as poets, by social roles, restraints, and expectations. They have lacked the prick of ambition, only very recently being required to say as little girls what they wanted to be when they grew up. Even for men, to declare poetic ambition has never been easy, but I remember the astonished envy I felt, as an adolescent growing up in Swansea, when a male contemporary said he intended to be a poet. To be anything, other than wife and mother, would be hard enough, but to want to be a poet showed a strange strong sense of self, power, and profession. Until this century, women have not only had no social backing and encouragement to be poets, but have lacked the advantage of education — the old classical education, involving reading and writing verse, was often a good start for poets of the right sex and class. Women have lacked solitude. Women have lacked professional confidence. Finally, as Musset's Muse may remind us, they have had less erotic freedom and flexibility than men. Hopkins says that feeling, love in particular, is the mainspring of poetry. Most women, as well as many men, have written passionate poetry in their teens and given it up on marriage. (Most working-class people of both sexes have never started.)

The women poets who adorn sixteenth-and seventeenth-century collections of verse tend to have titles. Queen Elizabeth wrote two good poems: one, 'The Daughter of Debate', about power and politics, another, 'Youth and Cupid', about a woman's regret for the rejected amorous chances of lost youth — it has a moving image, perhaps autobiographical, of plucked plumage. The Countess of Newcastle has a famous poem, 'The Soul's Garment', also about ageing, and another, 'The Sea Goddess', both strongly marked by cosmetic, ornamental, and domestic imagery from a woman's experience. Some poets wrote poetry which is not so obviously coloured by gender, like Lady Mary Wroath's beautiful lyric, 'Love, What Art Thou?' which no-one could sex on uninformed reading, and the Countess of Winchilsea's 'Jealousy', or 'On Love'. These are poems by great ladies possessing the advantage of education, leisure, wealth, social equality with men, and the freer erotic context of the court. As in Renaissance poetry by men, a special sexual knowledge and interest sometimes shows itself, sometimes not.

The history of English and American poetry is the history of male poets. (It is also the history of educated male poets.) No woman poet has made a historically marked significant contribution until the middle of our own century, with two exceptions which prove the rule. On our side of the Atlantic, Emily Brontë wrote a small amount of excellent, if not very varied, lyric poetry. On the other, Emily Dickinson unpublished in her lifetime on male advice, made a larger and more influential contribution. Both were spinsters, leading an intense secluded life, and both wrote a religious poetry with erotic feeling. They were eccentrically and valuably educated, repressed, solitary but in touch with cultivated companions and driven in on personal fantasy. Their singularity loudly draws our attention to the relative unimportance of other women poets before and in their time. They head a category of virginal, virginal-like, women poets marked by religious feeling, fantasy, and eccentricity — for instance, Christina Rossetti, Charlotte Mew, Stevie Smith. There is sometimes an excess of dottiness, sweetness, or softness in the personality of their work, partly attributable to sexual self-consciousness or distortion or social pressure. At their best they can be tough and tart, at their worst arch and frowsty, those old maids of poetry. Perhaps they may be related to the company of poetesses, Ella Wheeler Wilcox, Wilhelmina Stitch, and Patience Strong. Sometimes they have highly educated and creative fathers and brothers. Sometimes they work in secret. Sometimes their poetry seems unmistakably "feminine", sometimes it would be hard to sex. Charlotte Mew and Emily Dickinson wrote some poems which could be taken as men's poems. When I first read a poem by Emily Dickinson, in an account of studying literature in college by Jean Webster in *Daddy Long Legs* (a novel in which I also first met a critical view of *Jane Eyre*) it did not strike me as a woman's poem:

> I asked no other thing —
> No other — was denied —
> I offered Being — for it —
> The Mighty Merchant sneered —
>
> Brazil? He twirled a Button —
> Without a glance my way —
> "But — Madam — is there nothing else —
> That we can show — Today?"

Now it seems unmistakably a woman's poem, but the impression derives from a diffused knowledge of Emily Dickinsons's life and work, and it is not easy to say why the poem seems to be written by a woman. It draws on a sense of woman as passive consumer and customer; the Mighty Merchant is a marvellous image of contempt, courtesy, and power, one of a whole gallery of male images in women's poetry, like the beloved husband and less beloved masculine readers and critics in the verses of Anne Bradstreet, and Sylvia Plath's Daddy, Herr God, Lucifer, and Death.

Anne Bradstreet, Stevie Smith, and Sylvia Plath are all aware of the problem of a woman's Muse. (For Sapphic poets this is less worrying.) Mistress Bradstreet pointed out with typical mild clarity that it was unreasonable of men to see women's poetry as casual or stolen, since poetry was the offspring of Calliope, but anticipated their reply that myth was playful and fictitious. (We may well ponder the male-created images of female power — Muses, Fates, Furies, Sibyls, Pallas Athene. Men derived valuable images of irrationality from their invented, hysterical women.) Mistress Bradstreet became Muse, subject, and poetic colleague for a somewhat sexist poet, John Berryman, in what is one of his most successful poems. Stevie Smith was seriously flippant about her miserable Muse (looking like a Welsh witch in the drawing), managing to put her in her place as not wholly melancholy but only heard in the poet's blackest moods. Sylvia Plath found her Muse disquieting. A daughter tells a mother, in 'The Disquieting Muses', why ballet and piano lessons have not worked, while the stone ladies with stitched heads have, for better and for worse. This poem is a significant farewell to those ideals of accomplishment which finished off so many bright young ladies.

I have known some of Sylvia Plath's poems ('The Eyemote', for one) to be read as a man's writing, though most of the poetry after *The Colossus* is unmistakably sexed. Sylvia Plath strikes me, however, as a woman poet whose achievement is understandably but powerfully distorted by our mid-century feminism. The poetry feeds woman's political demands, needs, passions and eloquence from a poetic source which provides much more than the immediate nourishment for a hungry sisterhood. In 'Lady Lazarus', for instance, when we reach the ferocious declaration 'I eat men like air', the victims are established as Herr Doktor, Herr God, and Herr Lucifer, standing for a man-made culture, a man-made society, a man-made science, and a man-made religion. Its victims are, however, men and women. Similarly, in 'Nick and the Candlestick', a mother breathes prayers, protection and fears for her baby son, threatened by a poisoned and explosive future. The rage, compassion, love and hatred blaze as fuel for the woman's movement and for larger liberations.

Women's poetry is historically determined, and at present is frequently as doctrinaire as was the poetry of Byron, Shelley or the young Wordsworth. Women's poetry uses confession, crudity, candour, and aggression. It adds menstrual blood and cunts to the traditional erotic catalogue. It competes with the boasts and solicitations of rake's poetry. It rewrites the myths, images and assertions of men's poetry. When Adrienne Rich painfully quips, 'Every woman's death diminishes me', she deliberately diminishes a man's larger claim. 'Every man's death' is less sexually exclusive than 'every woman's'. The fight with a man's language, as we realise whenever we send a letter to a woman, is larger than the essays of poetic diction, but influences them and is influenced by them.

I want to acknowledge the feminist efforts in men's poetry, sometimes developing out of a traditionally limited contemplation of woman. Adrienne Rich sees the new women's poetry as destructive and creative, making new myths, knowing and uttering what she calls 'extraordinary forms of anger, joy, impatience, love and hope.' Men's poetry easily reveals the need for revisions and recreations. Tom McGrath, for instance, has a funny poem which admits that a poet is a jealous beast, using poetry as compensation for not making it

    . . . as a philosopher
or holyman or a jazz musician or a painter
or the mightiest lover or the politician.

It ends in an immodest putting-down of self: the poet writes love-poems about doing marvels with his angel-woman in bed while she is making it with a store detective. The woman-in-the-poem is a poetic sex-object. Male modesty might have better imagined and diagnosed — how about a woman not making it with any man, but making a poem? (The rivalry of literary mates is a huge subject of its own, not restricted to poetry, and gathering momentum daily.) Some poets move beyond the sex object in the poem. D.H. Lawrence, for one, and Yeats, for another, move away from socially patronising and aesthetic attitudes to women to imaginative impersonations of extra-ordinary anger, joy, impatience, love, and hope. What we ask, after all, of imagination, is that it should question the giver, imagine the other, chafe at the boundaries. Yeats grows from Helen of Troy to Crazy Jane. Like the speaker in Sylvia Plath's 'Daddy' and 'Lady Lazarus', his raging slut (who possessed him dangerously and had to be exorcised) attacks a man-made aesthetic, and a man-made society. She recreates sex, god, and language: "Love has pitched his mansion in the place of excrement". The new incarnation is an astounding achievement for Yeats, for feminism, for erotic freedom, and for poetry. A long step from his early poem, 'Adam's curse', where poets and women were all labouring to be beautiful.

Men and women exchange and inter-imagine myths. Ruth Fainlight worked on a series of poems about Sibyls in which she contemplates the life of a woman and an artist. The poems are good examples of imaginative essay through appropriate old and renewed myth but the Sibyls were in fact suggested by a man, Leonard Baskin, whose accompanying visual images also show a contemplation of sex and art. But perhaps the poetry of men and women has to draw apart for a time, like the lovers at the end of *Lady Chatterley*, the better to enjoy and understand copulations of body and mind.

There is a problem which I can only contemplate briefly. The masculine nature of English and American poetry is thrown into stong relief if we compare it with the history of prose fiction. You can't begin thinking about fiction without recognising the importance and originality of Fanny Burney, Jane Austen, the Brontës, Mrs Gaskell and George Eliot. While their sister poets were silent or weak enough to be suppressed, they changed the shape of their genre. Why? A few guesses and conjectures. At first sight, writing novels might seem harder to combine with the demands, stresses, and restrictions of a woman's social role. Would it not be easier to punctuate the dailiness of woman's housekeeping with lyric? Jane Austen pushed her manuscript under the blotting paper and greeted the caller. Mrs Gaskell worried about her novels, and her daughters' clothes and education, and was helped by her husband's prudent pocketing of royalties. Miss Evans/George Eliot had a male Muse, George Henry Lewes, lover, critic, buffer against reviewers, and literary agent. The novelists managed, one way and another. Why didn't more women poets write more deathless verses?

Does the poet, like the painter and composer, need solitude, space, and time in a special way? Does the poet require a social environment which promotes a sharp sense of the self? Is room of one's own, psychological and physical, more essential for the poet? Is domesticity more fatal, given the erotic and sensual nature of poetry and paint, to poet than to novelist, whose negative capabilities are more reconcilable, morally and practically, with what was, and for many still is, a woman's world? Keats's chameleon poet, drawn from the admiration of Shakespeare rather than from his own genius is, I believe, more like the novelist than the lyric poet. Although the novelist's art is one which demands a larger social concern, and might *prima facie* be better practised by men than women, we know that the woman novelist, even if housebound, has done wonders with microcosm and analogy. Men have, up to now, found it easier than women to find and combine the lute and the kiss, outside homes and houses. The egotistical sublime, Muse-supported and Muse-excited, has been masculine. Poetry — Donne's or Eliot's, or Yeats', or Plath's — shows a ceaseless, ruthless, egocentric demand for self-contemplation and self-creation. A woman character created by a man, the Marquise de Merteuil, in Laclos's novel, *Les Liasions Dangereuses,* speaks of creating herself. For her, and for men and women around her, the result was death, not art, but her need and purpose of self-creation show very clearly the need and purpose of poets, and her corrupted powers of making, imaginative and erotic, shed a fierce light on the difficulty of being a woman and a poet.

TOM PAULIN

On Rhyme

Some, though not most, of my poems rhyme and this is not because of a deliberate and conscious choice which I made as I was writing them. A poem shapes itself. For me it begins with a recognition, a surprise, and if I'm lucky I catch the cadence of a voice speaking. If an artificial division is made between form and content, style and subject, then the question can be asked: why does this poem rhyme? Why does that poem not rhyme? Very few literary critics bother to hear the poems they write about. Their ears are dead. What they are interested in is some neat little idea or some trim ambiguity. It is too easy to think of beauty as an object, a thing we can touch and examine and know. How can we ever know and understand the speaking voice? With its pauses, shadings, modulations and relishings it is a most various absolute, a gothic surprise. I do not think it is always lost in translation either — reading Clarence Brown's and W.S. Merwin's translation of Mandlestam I catch patterns of sound and find my lips moving. Though I know no Russian, I hope that I am glimpsing that "phonic surface" Clarence Brown speaks of.

In the language of institutions, in the official voices of bureaucrats, there is only hardness and rigidity. This is not the sort of voice I want to listen to. Some accents I hear are like acid in the ear, though I wonder when I react to them whether I am not holding to a vocal snobbery, and acoustic aestheticism. (The inverse of that attitude in members of an older generation which forced them to twist their provincial accents into a standard elocutionary voice.) Not so very long ago accents became fashionable, and I have met people who wish their voices were salted with tones that used to be regarded as hyperborean. But in all voices there is a playfulness, and now I can listen to the trills and coos in the Oxford voice with pleasure — at least sometimes, in some people. Those gritty, practical voices — the voices of ambitious bureaucrats and powerful men — the spirit is dead in their tones. It is like hearing grey steel and washed-out flannel talking. Again, we mustn't forget how useful and seductive an accent can be: when Stalin phoned Pasternak to ask if he should spare Mandlestam he spoke in a distinctively Georgian accent. How many of his future victims trusted that voice?

We can imagine the soul as light moving, or we can hear each soul as a unique voice that exists beyond the tyranny of the simply visual. It is like a choice between photographs — those 'inventories of mortality' — and the living sounds of a voice. And though the editor asked for an unpublished poem, I feel that one I have already published might make my answer clearer. The photographs are invisible in the twilight and I am hoping to hear certain voices. This poem rhymes — for a change.

Firelight

Framed among ornaments, one by one
you've started to become
the faces of dead people — those
who died young, who made nothing
happen outside us, and the old
seated in armchairs like thrones,
prepared to die, but smiling.
It closed in, like the evenings
silting the tall windows.
Your voices brimmed here, but now,
dead ones, I visit you with those
glances we know. Ask me how
we got to this firelight and I'll sing
in your voices, softly, of absences.

The imperative to listen which is so often a strategy in rhetoric and argument can be transformed into the gentlest demand to open our ears to the richness of voices, to hear and love them.

JEAN EARLE

The Woollen Mill

What we are hangs upon that moment —
Which *will* come —
When the cross is taken in the warp
And the weave is certain.

On the drying-ground where the wet wools
Are hung to blow,
Scarlet and blue,
I was first aware of my true pattern

To do with light . . .

It was an overwhelming addition to myself
To see prepared in light how the warp lay.
I had to go in and sit down behind the carder,
Trying to cope!

In the pile of fluff lay a dog, asleep.
Along his half-closed lids
Light sparkled, even there, in the dreaming eye.

On the walls, white light translated
Water, the roaring silver
Over the wheel — that groaned out light — and light —
Danced from the ancient cogs, from when they were young wood.

Such bright looking hurt. When someone passed,
I turned my head for relief of his shadow.
But he left two fish on the window sill
And they burned light: drew it into their stillness
Like a great cry. Blinding silver.

The man dressing a loom was all afire
With fused intent, passing down arms and fingers
Into his skilful moves.
As in a thrown shuttle, I watched the visible mix
Between his light of mind and the silverlit water
Working outside.
At that time, the mill was run by water —
In dry weather, the wheel stopped.
But then, against such interval,
A mountain of wool was dyed,
Scarlet, blue —
Blown through the thirsty, rounding light
So that, when rain came
And the wheel turned,
There would be plenty of warp ready to take the cross.

It was the season when the natterjack goes to the water
Carrying her mate —
Or so they did on my far-back nameday —

And as they processed,
All the light in the sky *flew*
To touch flashpoints at the stream's edge
Where the webbed feet displaced moisture,
Tilted instant mirrors,
Killing all dark places between flowers,
Marsh buttercups: and those fill up with light
Even in thunder.

Look back, from evening . . .

A widespread day, maddened yet silked with light.
Wool blowing unbearable keen colours,
Toads assembling —
The two fish, burning.

Those were taken home by the weaver
To his shut house. The mill shut down.

A pink light came delicately on
So that the many truths
Flushed into one.

The cross taken.

GILLIAN CLARKE

Plums

When their time comes they fall
without wind, without rain.
They seep through the trees' muslin
in a slow fermentation.

Daily the low sun warms them
in a late love that is sweeter
than summer. In bed at night
we hear heartbeat of fruitfall.

The secretive slugs crawl home
to the burst honeys, are found
in the morning mouth on mouth,
inseparable.

We spread patchwork counterpanes
for a clean catch. Baskets fill,
never before such harvest,
such a hunter's moon burning

the hawthorns, drunk on syrups
that are richer by night
when spiders are pitching
tents in the wet grass.

This morning the red sun
is opening like a rose
on our white wall, prints there
the fishbone shadow of a fern.

The early blackbirds fly
guilty from a dawn haul
of fallen fruit. We too
breakfast on sweetnesses.

Soon plum trees will be bone,
grown delicate with frost's
formalities. Their black
angles will tear the snow.

ALAN LLWYD

Gwyddau

Fe'u clywid, ar drothwy'r Calan, yn gwichian yn goch
yn y stabl, a'u hadenydd yn curo'n stond
ym mhang eu hangau,
a'r gwaed, wrth ddiferu o geudwll,
yn llifo'n drochion o dan y drws.

Yn ddiniwed o'u tynged hwy,
fe'u gwelid yn torsythu ar fuarth
a chaeau'r fferm, neu'n ochri eu ffordd
yn osgordd faldorddus, hurt;
hen wyddau tafodrydd-feddw
yn clegar fel hen wragedd ffraegar mewn ffrwgwd
heb lestair ar eu parabl ystwyth,
a'u hystum yn llawn trahauster;
gwyddau wrth eu boddau mewn pydewau dŵr,
neu'n pori'r maestir am oes.

Fe'u hysid fesul un
o'r cae, wrth i'r cŵn
eu herlid; gwyrid y gwar
hyblyg yn lleithder y stabl,
ei wyro cyn plycio'r plu
nes bod yr ŵydd ddwyflwydd oed
yn gwichian a hisian fel bagbib yng nghesail
fy nhad, cyn i lafn oer
ei siswrn grafu drwy'r asgwrn yn drwsgl,
ac agor twll yn y corun.

Gerfydd eu traed rhoed y gwyddau gwarfain
i hongian yn rhengoedd
llipa a swrth; buom ninnau wrthi,
hyd hwyr y nos, yn eu trin hwy,
ac yn tynnu'r corblu o'r cyrff
nes bod y lluwchfeydd ysbeidiol yn llenwi'r lle,

a phob archoll yn staenio llawr y stabl,
a'r plu'n ymgymysgu â'r gwaed
fel ewyn gwyn gan fachlud yn goch,
ac wedi eu pluo i gyd
eu rhoi'n noeth ar y glorian wag.

Ar doriad y wawr
drannoeth, yr oedd llwydrew Ionawr
fel plu yn gwaedu i gyd.

Geese

On New Year's Eve, one could hear their red scream
in the stable, and the wings beating still
in the grasp of death,
and the blood, dripping from a round hole,
flowed like foam under the door.

Innocent of their fate,
they could be seen swaggering on the farmyard
and on the fields, or waddling
in a stupid, babbling host;
loose-tongued, drunken geese
cackling like quarrelsome old women,
their supple speech without restraint,
and their postures arrogant;
geese grazing in the fields for a lifetime
or paddling in pools.

One by one they would be pursued
from the field, set on by dogs;
the flexible nape would be bent
in the damp stable,
bent before feathers were plucked,
and the young goose
hissed and screamed like bagpipes in my father's
armpit, before the cold blade
of his scissors scraped clumsily through the bone,
and opened a hole in the head.

The thin-naped geese dangled by their feet
as limp as clothes on the clothes-line;
it took us to nightfall
plucking the feathers and scorching the skin,
and the snatched snow grew on the ground;
the stable's floor was stained by wounds,
and the feathers, mingling with the blood,
were as white foam fuming red in the sunset,
and scoured, they were placed on the scales.

On the break of dawn the next day
the hoarfrost of January
bled like feathers.

(Translated by the author)

CHRISTOPHER MEREDITH

Jets

All day the jets have rifled through the air,
Drilled through the lessons that I've tried to give,
Scabbing the blue with vapour for a scar,
Passing the dummy-bombed hamlets with a wave.

I've comforted myself. I'm not so bad,
I've thought, in spite of the raised voice, the sudden squall —
If discipline and strictness knocks them dead
At least I'm not out there learning to kill.

And each frail cliché rears to the surface,
Writhes in the strong light, dies, and having sunk
Leaves me to know I work for who in office
Shuts books to put more octane in the tank.

What I would does not possess our minds.
This boy, the fat one, has been rifled too,
Belongs to the plane and every bomb it sends,
Absorption melted from his ragged row

Of words. Just now, he, my bluntest blade
Inevitably felled first in any game,
Looked from the tortured page, the word-wrought board,
To a sky where steel hammered its own scream —
And smiled.

MIKE JENKINS

"He Loved Light, Freedom & Animals"

(An inscription on the grave of one of the children who died in
the Aberfan disaster of October 21, 1966.)

No grave could contain him.
He will always be young
in the classroom
waving an answer
like a greeting.

Buried alive —
alive he is
by the river
skimming stones down
the path of the sun.

When the tumour on the hillside
burst and the black blood
of coal drowned him,
he ran forever
with his sheepdog leaping
for sticks, tumbling together
in windblown abandon.

I gulp back tears
because of a notion of mànliness.
After the October rain
the slag-heap sagged
its greedy belly.
He drew a picture of a wren,
his favourite bird for frailty
and determination. His eyes gleamed
as gorse-flowers do now
above the village.

His scream was stopped mid-flight.
Black and blemished
with the hill's sickness
he must have been,
like a child collier
dragged out of one of Bute's mines.

There he is, climbing a tree
mimicking an ape, calling names
at classmates. Laughs springing
down the slope. My wife hears them
her ears attuned as an ewe's in lambing,
and I try to foster the inscription,
away from its stubborn stone.

SHEENAGH PUGH

I Think Someone Might Write An Elegy

I think someone might write an elegy
for the dead words; the shapely words
that have no shape to fit round now,
whose ladies have stepped out of them,
as it were, and left them in a huddle,
the words we don't have things for. I think
someone might write an elegy for words

like timothy, cocksfoot, feverfew,
fennel and saffron, ginger and galingale.
For mowdewart and marmot; for furze-pig
and parmaceti; for feline
and anserine; for Lawrence the tod.
For cirrus, nimbus and stratocumulus.
For Persepolis, Hamadan, Shushan,
for Tolleshunt d'Arcy and Cirencester;
for Elizabeth Sarah Davidson,
which once seemed to me the fairest words
that ever anyone laid tongue to.
For the words that mean nothing now
and whose loveliness, made as it was
by what they meant, has left them; the husks
of dragonflies, drying out . . . Things that are dead
we keep with words, but when the words die
themselves; oh then they're dead, and dead indeed.

GEOFFREY HOLLOWAY

Severn Minnows

In the sun's strobe their quick silver
looks random as spilt nails,
yet each moves with acute control;
never touching, however curt
the space between.

They were the totems, devout toys
of my Shropshire childhood:
ambushed in pouncy nets and jars
they gleamed, spiralled its open rooms,
its radiant sills.

'They won't keep, you know,' said grownups.
I used to try, four days —
but could never win, before time
unforgivably some white gut
would surface, stop.

They were here when the troop trains went
— shoals flashing bayonets —
when the spare, khaki ghosts came back,
in and out of their smashed, wet skulls
like loose shrapnel.

They are here now, in the Bren's brisk
tock from Copthorne Barracks
— sound of a butcher chopping meat —
with no swans, only a river
lead-ripped, sad.

RICHARD POOLE

A Meditation After Love

Lying beside you after love,
I found my hand cupping the flesh
that softens the jut of your hip:
caressing it, I felt it move,
slide and stretch like a flattened strip
of rubber bedded on the bone —
the soft and hard, as over stone
goes water's supple, silken mesh.

Love, it delighted me to see
in these contingent qualities
the termini of your nature:
in one the liquid pliancy

of a sympathetic creature;
the other an image of will
fixed, obdurate, immovable:
the heart's and mind's polarities.

How difficult it is to love
you wholly, continually,
you who are never singular,
whose nature moves as the clouds move,
altering, never regular:
to love what is unsensual
and what is uncongenial:
to love in the bone, finally.

Perhaps it is impossible,
a mere Platonic idea,
an ache of imagination:
it is commonplace to settle
for that slow accommodation
which defines a working marriage —
two people caged in a glass cage
of habit, and one another.

Time, love, is both our enemy
and our abettor: to compose
time's rhythm we must now move apart
and now together, here hurry
there dawdle, conclude and re-start,
see the common and the strange fill
our lives up like a bag — there will
be sharp thorns, and sometimes a rose.

One another's familiars,
old associates of the flesh,
often side by side we lie still:
contented to lie thus, heedless
of the unknown hour that will kill,
sweeping passion, indifference,
our world from the world, and sentence
our bodies to the earth's black crèche.

The dead, love, neither dream nor stir:
the sharp worm and the sharp maggot
pierce them through with never an itch,
the fat needles of a sempster
whose only art is to unstitch:
impossible to blunt their will —
these lovers do not stop until
the last bone is immaculate.

Beneath your flesh I touch the bone,
through that which yields, that which defies:
qualities which are contrary —
one water-soft, one hard like stone —
yet also complementary,
for one softens what one defines,
one underlies what one confines —
till that which animates them dies.

RUTH BIDGOOD

Edward Bach Advises His Sister

(A found poem from a letter of 1802, written from Ludlow)

Dear Sister,
Although I have no reason
to suspect you of misconduct,
yet my affection and solicitude
will, I hope, excuse these lines
of brotherly advice.
Being visited by men
who profess themselves your admirers,
and not under the protection of your parents,
you are now at the most critical period
in the life of a woman.

Young, inexperienced, unsuspicious,
fond of flattery (as what woman is not),
she too often falls a victim to those worst of men
who, with the aid of oaths, protestations,
and promise of marriage,
seduce her from the paths of virtue,
rob her of her virginity,
and leave her to lament her credulity
in the most abject state of wretchedness,
deserted by her acquaintance,
reviled and scoffed at by her enemies,
a reproach to her friends,
a disgrace to her family,
and, far worse than all these,
condemned by her own conscience!
The remainder of her life
must be miserable indeed.

If ever you find yourself in danger
of falling into this pit,
think only of the picture I have drawn
and you will shrink with horror
from the dreadful prospect,
and reflect with pleasing terror
on your happy deliverance
from the jaws of a monster so hideous.

Again, dear sister, let me advise you
not to throw yourself away.
You are yet very young,
neither ugly nor deformed,
of a creditable family,
and not entirely destitute of fortune.
Not that I would have you consider yourself
of more consequence than you are,
but I would deter you from doing
that which is beneath you.
Your very affectionate Brother,
Edward Bach.

R. S. THOMAS

Feminine Gender

It has the elusiveness
of great art: the poem
so near, unwilling to be written.
I have knocked all these years
at the door of a supposed house
with somebody inside
(the movement of a curtain)
who refuses to answer.
            Sometimes
as a face in chapel
it has appeared, raven-haired,
sallow of cheek, staring
through locked fingers. I waited
to have speech with it after
and it was gone.
            Mostly
it was the shadow of a bent
woman, too old to believe in, disfiguring
my sunlight.
            Was she ever
a young girl, as innocent
as compelling, before history submerged
her in the anonymity
of the valleys?
            Some must have known
her so, giving her a name
to live for, to die for, and a language
like seed corn, coming to harvest
again, as often as it is cut down.

STEVE GRIFFITHS

Guardianship

Around the walls pebbled with violent glass
set in cement
to save values from vandals
the insomniac blood roams
like a fox watching fire
that comforts
fox-people with brilliant implements
and edgy thoughts.

It is easy to see the provision
of any order as a saving grace,
my desk as a liner in savage lightless seas,
shedding the reassurance of its cabins' trim
on the gaping, clashing rooves of the waves,
cherishing the machinery,
the possible,
for want of another principle.

I do what I am paid to do
at my desk with my computer terminal:
they can rustle my outward papers,
the Vandals and Huns, when they burst in —
brimming with red-eyed fecklessness,
their cleavers flecked —
for I have inviolate information.
I have done relatively well.

They break the bulbs of neighbours' passageways,
strike out each other's eyes.
To abandon your luggage is a fool's game.
Observing the convention,
I do not speak of those who never had it.
Each is a radio in a lonely cubicle.
I read the morning papers with ferocity
to stem the snapping ideological tide.

The blood puts its voice in a mixer,
crowds, buzzes.
It flows down to the hallucinatory green
of the pitch, like a spillage
wanting to eat the stars,
pawing them,
those cuts of meat left
upright in socks,
their fast convertible health,
a meat-eaters' carnival.

PETER THABIT JONES

They Thought

They thought I was wooden:
They tried to nail me.
I changed into a boat:
They tried to sail me.
I sunk to the bottom as a rock:
They came down with hammers: knock, knock, knock.

They thought I was bleeding:
They kicked and stabbed me.
I changed into a shark:
They tried to grab me.
I spat out of the water as a jet:
They came after me, their frowns set.

They thought I had a bomb:
They tried to ignite me.
I changed into a balloon:
They tried to bite me.
I hit the green ground as a fast fox:
They brought out their dogs and wire-box.

They thought I spread disease:
The tried to inject me.
I changed into a hole:
They tried to detect me.
I lay all dark; lay all alone:
They covered my opening with a stone.

S. C. LAPINGTON

Sea Litter

All day on a thinning margin, the hiss
of receding, the crush of wave folding;
dead pause between. Planetary pulse.
And globs of oil, lard-tubs, the planking

of snapped boats, letterless bottles,
old hawsers — anacondas — stiff with tar.
Litter, fragments, ruined on a shore.
And shoes, colours salted out, curled

tongues and soles; though never a pair
of the rotting leathers, buoyant plastics;
nor a body to tell the loss — of strugglers
in the water, of lovers on the strand,

relinquishing. Only a slicked gull
and a sheep off the cliff. And a sea run
in the while, a vast and formless flow,
an intuition, craving, dreading, by turns.

The cork flares, the plastics melt into
noxious polyps, sand into glass; aerosols
detonate. And tomorrow, ashes doused, fresh
corrugations as if a huge chain drags.

179

GLYN JONES

The Meaning Of Fuchsias

The lush valley, the two golden mares
    loving in the apple orchard,
 The golden-maned for Gwilym, the milky one
  for me,
And through those dark boughs the vast white
    mansion-walls of heaven.
 Why did we not hear, in that treachery
  of sun-varnished windows,
Of handsome clouds, of the fragrant flesh of pears,
    of gull-white moons in their eternal blue,
 And pastures cast out of morning fire
  everywhere brilliant as enamels,
The creeping by of our days, of our time,
    of change —
 Only the thrush's hammering of morning
  in the dapples of that sunlight,
And the cupboards of the trees around us,
    creaking, creaking.

On the slope the still bushes stood in the sun,
    staring down in silence at their shadows.
 "Fuchsias", said Gwilym, "wild fuchsias" —
  each bush of flowers
The dark glow in my mind still of lit lanterns
    burning crimson through transparencies of wine,
 A new delight then, inextinguishable,
  a heart's enduring wonder.

In these sleek gardens, where only meaning
    has no root or blossoming,
 What is it within me stares through its bars
  at fuchsias,
So that I bear again the sudden burden
    of my many dead,

And you, and all our darkened suns,
    possess me through the doorways of my tears,
You, sanctified listener, who rode by night
      your golden pony
  Through the graveyard, listening,
    And hearing nothing.

JOYCE HERBERT

The Coming

When the roof trusses came
they were an Ark growing up from the lorry,
a forest cut down but living still.

The lorry moved reverently
accepting tributes
from the branches of trees in the lane,
so that leaves hung once more from the beams.

The builders waved, cheered,
stood to welcome it, smiling at each other.
The carpenter, as High Priest,
plucked the first beam.

All the air smelt of resin
when they carried the timbers in,
stacked them ready for the roof
where they would sign their names secretly, as makers,
high above the house
where they were most at ease.

SUE MOULES

Men

It is Summer,
I dress sparsely
To counteract heat.
Young men whistle from inside
The glass front of a converted shop.
I walk on blushed.
In the bakery
A middle-aged man
Traces his finger down my tanned back
Dipping under the dress rouching.
I cannot spurt out my anger
For he is a citizen.
Walking home
Heavy with shopping,
A little old man
From the old people's home
Stops, takes off his straw hat,
Bows low,
Wishes me a good morning.

ELWYN DAVIES

Lumber Collectors

They are big-muscled scavengers
hanging on their prowling lorry
like Gestapo thugs after Jews.

Outside a house where terminal
breakage or dislike or a bit
extra in the bank has put paid

to old furniture now huddled
on the pavement they stop and crowd
round as if making an arrest.

They sort and manhandle the stuff
and drag it and throw it aboard.
It no longer rates gentleness.

They say, "What people chuck away
these days. I could use that myself."

But they have no skill to discuss
(though the woman at the window,
an informer at a pogrom,
sees the removal and recalls)
the marking with vomit, ink, wine,
sperm, coffee, piss and on the sofa
enough grease for a cake of soap;
still less the hands that touched, the eyes
that rested on these artefacts,
the bodies they supported awake or
asleep, sitting, fucking or dead;
and least of all those emanations
of wordless bitter-sweet nothings,
the smells of extinct joy or pain
or being things used are fraught with,
influences and infections
so fugitive no dog could track them.

CHRISTINE EVANS

Off Camera

It is comparisons with Eden, effusions
on the quietness of Enlli,
that make them smile off camera,
the islanders returned by helicopter
to their birthplace for the day. Their faces say
this place was nothing special,
more than all the hidden countries
of our childhood. The interviewer wants
hiraeth, the echoes of old loss
or an Ishmael resentment
to engage the audience and justify
his budget. But they do not seem
particularly thrilled
by the trick of sweeping back so smoothly. Even today
this white-ringed island is not inaccessible
to them: it is a real place
their minds return to regularly as the birds
to breed; the enduring pole
they measure progress from.
It is the mainland, they point out, themselves,
that have moved on.

BRYAN ASPDEN

Erw Fawr

A slice of candied fruit is served
On top of each gatepost this frosty morning.
White knitting unravels from a drain;
And blinkered cars limp along the road
While I walk Mot past the entrance
To Erw Fawr, the estate we've watched grow

From an early sowing of breeze blocks
To streetlamps fruiting on concrete stalks;

Past crimped fields, pokerwork hedges,
Ivy dressed in crusaders' armour;
Cracked plasterboard dumped among the ragwort
Where voles ring little bells: "Blind, blind!"
As the day owl, pasty-faced,
Comes kerbcrawling by.

You know the place I mean: its culture
Of small dogs, half coconuts, the nurseryman's
Favourite escallonia, "Apple Blossom";
Lawns brisk with cypress bollards; and merrygorounds
Of washing? A nice place
To build a greenhouse after Manchester:
Where Stan and Connie, Con and Stanley
Petition for the planting of trees?

We live across the way. The corner site,
With the bent aerial, the sales-model Citroen
Visa; rhododendrons cringing in the wind,
Sick of their diet of limestone chips;
Our two children; our two tongues; our two
Remaining hens, and their rare eggs.

NEAL MASON

The Holiday Brochure

The holiday brochure shines
its sixty watt reflection on his skin,
dank suburbs forgotten as he basks
by a glossy blue sea, pours a glass
of pure spring water from a bottle,
twopence off at Sainsbury's, lays himself down
like a bath-towel on a beach.

The mountains stretch away
far beyond the battered chair, the grey
smoke-filled room cloudless
as distant eagles whirl
slowly round the lampshade and,
when he wants an olive, he need only
reach out and pick one.

Too hot with both bars on
he leans to switch one off, feels the heat
beating on his face while, down in the street,
a mule train plods past, hot sand
simmering the sound, golden granules
soft to his touch as liquid sunlight
or a shag-pile rug.

Curled against the cold his threadbare cat
sleeps on unaware of wolves baying
from beyond the divan, the snow-capped
mantelpiece echoing their calls as the sun
sinks back into its brochure;
outside a cold clatter of milk bottles
rattling on the doorstep of night.

ZBIGNIEW HERBERT

Pan Cogito On Virtue

1.

It's not surprising
she is not the bride
of real men

generals
strongmen
despots

they are followed down the ages
by that weepy old maid
in a terrible Salvation Army bonnet
who nags

she fetches a portrait of Socrates
from an old lumber-room
a cross kneaded in bread
old words

— while all around a splendid life roars
pink like an abattoir at dawn

one could almost bury her
in a silver casket
of innocent souvenirs

she shrinks
like hair in the throat
like a buzz in the ear

2.

My God
if only she were a little younger
and prettier

marched with the spirit of the times
swung her hips
to the beat of fashionable music

perhaps real men would then
fall in love with her
generals strongmen despots

if only she took more care
looked human
like Liz Taylor
or the Goddess of Victory

but she stinks of
mothballs
her lips are sealed
she reiterates the great No

insufferably stubborn
comic like a scarecrow
like an anarchist's dream
like the lives of saints

Translated from the Polish by Adam Czerniawski

DUNCAN BUSH

Cold-Chisel

Cold-
chisel; bar; hexagon
of steel,
    you
put pressure
to the world through
a hammer-blow earthed
through a fist —

    searching
for the weak
point
in old, reverberant
brickwork, for
    fulcrum: to shatter

or prise,
    or flake
superfluity of marble to
    shape

out of a litter
of white chippings, and,
      angled, chase
the finest crease of skin under an eyelid.

Dropped, you clink.
You are the thing
that nothing hammers flat.

Blunt
or delicate,
by need,
   you
form and dismantle,
like good writing
should:
    cold-chisel.

HUW JONES

Lullaby

Lanes are lost
beneath the leaves
my child
beneath the leaves
and swallows part
with speed and grace
under an amber sky.

The ragged trees
have turned to mist
my child
turned to mist
and badgers leave
their secret beds
to hunt in hooting woods.

Stars are steps
above the hill
my child
above the hill,
the moon a slide
for you to slip
with animals and birds.

ALISON BIELSKI

white lady song

Oystermouth castle, Gower

wishing post
whipping post
I stick my pin
let human dust
from the past
rising begin

to form your shape
bring me fresh hope
as I prepare
to rebuild love
not lapse or weave
webs of despair
      nine times circle the post
      dance and wish for what is lost

with you I stand
on blooded ground
sharing your pain
now let desire
surge and require
my full return

to confidence
as strong defence
when sensitive
for you must know
each verbal blow
causes me grief
        nine times circle the post·
        dance and wish for what is lost

you turn your back
that naked shock
cuts to the core
with bleeding weals
that nothing heals
you fade into the door

DANNIE ABSE

Bloody Horse

You can't quite
identify it
the long straight road
unsignposted
zipping between hedges
to a scandalously
gorgeous sunset.
As you look closer
shading your eyes
with your right hand
vigilant you'll see
the visitant
the white horse
half way down it.

Do you remember?
Your father drove the car
the family squabbling
this way years ago
many a time
this Roman road
that's empty now
but for the distant
truant pink horse
with a barely
visible
red shadow
racing towards
the signals of sunset.

War-high in the sky
vapour trails fatten
and you know again
the common sense
of déjà vu. Perhaps
someone far from home
should be playing
a mouth organ
a melody slow
and sad and wanton
a tune you've heard
but can't quite say
as the purple horse
surprises the sunset.

And you close your eyes
trying to name it all.
But you recall only
the day's small prose
certain queachy things
what the office said
what the office did
as the sunset goes

as the black horse goes
into the darkness.
And you forget
how from the skin
below your thumbnail
your own moon rises.

CHRISTINE EVANS

Out Of The Dark

I am the last night of August, late.
Under the sycamores darkness is so full
it cannot sleep. Four fields away the sea
dreams of suffocation.
The barley's schoolgirl heads
are bowed and waiting.

I am globular and slow.
My pores ooze salt and honeydew.
There is red wine still
at the corners of my mouth.
I feel the white rose arching to the moment
her petals peel and fall.

Ripe flesh hangs heavy;
drags back to the earth.

Towards dawn, I turn into a fat pale moth
blundering through cowbreath air
pressing myself against windows
seeking cracks in bedroom doors
to let slip the petals of my wings
where winter will not scatter them
before they are read.

In sea and trees and barley
and in your twisted sheets
I sweat and sigh.

I am the pause
between filling and flowing
the hush
at the heart of bursting
I am all roundness
beginning to wrinkle
to blur at the edges with fever
to pucker and seep
and I ache to be sharpened
to be picked, to be eaten
sliced back to the core
by a breath of the Arctic

rubbed clean like a new moon
to be angular, lithe
to be thin as a flash
windblown and buried

to be quickened

To come out of the dark
breathing clear horizons, wider skies

To be September.

MIKE JENKINS

Invisible Times

Living in invisible times:
loneliness an economist's art.

Into the phone I take care:
testing the colour of each word

because of the spy whose wire
antennaes twitch, whose mouth
is a metal tube my voice falls down
to be shred like paper.

Outside, I wear a crustaceous coat,
knowing that the rain avenges
those gun-barrel chimneys
who wage war on the sky.
One day my scales will be eaten away
and flesh frazzle to cinders.

All around are the sick people
who cannot find the germs.
I tell them where to look:
under switches which grow on fingertips,
in clocks whose hands are trees
and pylons and flags.

Every day I'm on this journey:
looking for the computer who told
those lies, who caused my rejection.
"Facts are seeds grown hard
as bullets", I would inform it.
But my search is aimless,
because the computer whirrs
in too many skulls to crack open.

The expert tells me I'm mad.
I see the motorway that workmen
are laying behind his grin:
it runs from the city of emotion
to the city of reason
and all purpose is within its rims.

DUNCAN BUSH

The Sea, The Sea

Lavernock was not only a place I used to go to, it was a
paradigmatic experience in time; it was a crystallisation of the
always-irrecoverable past.

It was those early Sunday mornings in summer, still cool
before the heat, and a press of families standing on the platform
at Llandaff North station waiting for a train that was already half-
full, and that would be packed to standing room only by the time
it left Grangetown, two stops later. It was the 'Yankee comic' I
had been bought at a newsagents for the journey — a 'Lash
LaRue' perhaps, or a 'Pecos Bill'. Then, when the train finally
reached the little station at Lavernock — two platforms and a
cream picket fence at the edge of a hayfield — it was the halfmile
walk down that country lane between the fields to reach the
beach, the crowd now strung out, as on a pilgrimage.

This of course was the middle Fifties: the halcyon days before
diesel trains, before Beeching. They were compartment trains,
without corridors, and the seats had a dusty reek never
encountered since. Above were luggage racks of netted cord, like
hammocks, and a foxed mirror between those sempiternally
sunny monochromes of Great Yarmouth or the Wye at Symonds
Yat. To lower the window you tugged, and released, a leather
belt like a razor strop; and when you thrust out your abruptly
windblown head — only one of many infant heads along your
side of the swaying train — you had to keep your eyes screwed up
when looking front in case of specks of hot coal in the warm,
blustery slipstream buffeting your face.

This was also a time when few members of the working class
owned cars, which meant that other places on the coast —
Llantwit Major or Ogmore or St Donat's say — were out of
reach. The trains didn't go there, and it was too far to cycle. You
might get to Llantwit or Ogmore once a year, on the back of the
lorry in the 'Whitsun Treat'. But otherwise — if you lived in
Cardiff, at least — you went unfailingly to Lavernock. People
'from the Valleys' (i.e. anywhere north of Tongwynlais) were

rumoured to prefer Barry Island, however: overcrowded, crass, commercialised, expensive Barry. (The reasons for this were unknown, but had, presumably, to do with that general cultural benightedness and gullibility attributed by all city-dwellers to those who live in the hinterland. Actually, it was probably a matter of which local rail line you were on for the coast.)

Lavernock, in any case, was much more basic. True, there was the nautically-named 'Golden Hind', a members-only drinking club. But apart from this, when you came off the country road, it was just a dust-and-gravel pathway down among the trees, the exposed roots of which were shiny from decades of footsoles. Then there were a couple of white-painted wooden shacks; these were boarded up and empty for seven or eight months of the year, but in the summer they sold the usual necessities: icecreams, tin buckets and spades, rainbow-whorled rubber balls, pink candyfloss, more Yankee comics, sandwiches and teas (with large deposit against return of teapot, cups, spoon, tray, etc.). There were also a pair of vile, fly-murmurous 'toilets' — latrine-sheds that led, it was believed, directly into the rusty, half-buried sewage pipe that ran a little way down the upper part of the beach before disappearing into the sand, only to debouch, presumably, somewhere out in the Channel. In any case, I — and I assume, most people — rarely used this amenity. We would simply wade out for another swim instead, on the cynical, urban assumption — almost certainly correct — that it would all end up there anyway.

When the tide was right out the beach, on the right-hand side, was a promontory of seaweed and grey mud, then rocks and rock pools. In the middle, far out, were rippled sandbanks and marooned lagoons. Higher up, though, there was usually a sufficient area of flat, hard sand to permit the bare-chested football game that seemed always to be in progress and that, as an onlooker, I remember as always involving full teams, a nearly full-sized pitch, an almost professional degree of sweat and combativeness and, in fact, one or two players who were 'on the City's books'. These games seemed to cease only when the tide was right in, whereupon the beach became suddenly almost as packed as the succession of trains which had supplied it. This was the time to take out the last few sandwiches — which had become compressed in the bag — and the second flask of tea. Even the kids and the tireless, obsessive football-players would be forced either to go in for a swim or, finally, sit with everyone else on the narrow strip of rocks and round grey pebbles at the foot of the cliffs, watching the sunlit brown waves rise and break a few yards from your feet.

Later on in the fifties, my family acquired its own transport — a green van — and we began to go further along the coast on these Sunday outings: to Llantwit, mostly. But for some reason I began to feel more out of things on these trips. I suppose I was the forerunner of someone I later wrote a poem about:

> A morose
> solitary child, too old for his parents,
> slumps in the back seat at a lay-by, watches
> the cars blur past . . .

It wasn't just a question of my age. Places like Llantwit and Ogmore always had a faintly genteel air, one of Morris estate cars and primuses and tablecloths spread on the grass; and everybody parked, and sat, as far as possible from everybody else. What I missed was the proletarian populousness, or intimacy, or coarseness, or whatever it was, of Lavernock. And it occurs to me only now that those born after the Fifties in Cardiff will probably never realise how important 'going down the bay' was in the city's culture: part of a simultaneously marine and urban culture that has always seemed to me as profanely physical and open air as that of Camus' Oran, as tough and streetwise as that of Pasolini's Rome.

Of course, that Lavernock is gone now. Trains no longer stop at the little station, and the fields at the top of the cliff above the beach are now a large caravan park. And, since whoever owns these fields also owns access — or at least parking — this beach too has now effectively been privatised. Ironically, I suppose, many of the caravans seem to be owned by Cardiffians of about my own age who, doubtless, once came there as kids, on the train from Llandaff North or Cardiff General or Grangetown, just as I did. Do they, too, miss the old Lavernock? I doubt it. In some ways — at least, financially — they are better off than their parents were in the Fifties. They have the cars and the caravans their parents didn't, and why not? Probably it was only living away that made the place, and that period, so important in my memory. There is, after all, in some a nostalgia for the demotic just as surely as there is, in others, for the aristocratic.

Anyway, when my wife and first son and I came back to South Wales, to St Donat's, in the summer of 1982, I saw that what *was* still here, what hadn't changed, was the coastline and the cliffs, and not just at Lavernock but all along that familiar wavering bulge just west of the inlet that is Cardiff on the map: those eroding grey-and-yellow limestone cliffs barred horizontally with strata, like the breast of the honey-buzzard in the birdbook. I was thirty-five years old — half the biblical span; and I felt it had taken all of that for those cliffs to show through in me, as a rock formation wears through topsoil.

And of course there was the sea itself. The sea has always been important to the imaginative life of South Walians: not only because of a maritime past, and the stories which came out of that, but because of ordinary but ineradicable private memories, like those I'm writing about here, and which all littoral peoples share. Perhaps this sense is best expressed by the exultant massed shout of 'Thalassa! Thalassa!' in Xenophon when, after weeks of travelling, the sea is finally descried; and any kid who has ever been to Lavernock or Barry or Porthcawl on a summer daytrip will have experienced that moment too. Here, of course, it is no wine-dark Aegean that we confront but, often enough, that cement-grey gleam of the Bristol Channel under a wash of low cloud. But that instant of simultaneous expectedness and surprise, that slight lift to the heart, remains the same; and I experience it undiminished now — and almost every day, I suppose — at St Donat's when, at certain points of the road or turns in the driveways, suddenly the sea, and on a clear day Devon, are glimpsed across the last fields.

ANTHONY CONRAN

Thirteen Ways Of Looking At A Hoover

For Barbara Zanditon

I

The party suddenly condensed
To the four of us —
Him, and him and her, and me.

I have never seen anger so elegant!
He checkmates them
Lifting their legs
To hoover, ruthlessly, their chair-space.

II

A hoover is like a camel —
It humps itself with provender
And can be trained to spit.

III

One would hardly believe
That even four humans and two cats
Gave so much skin.

Yet, once a week,
The bloated paper intestine of this beast
Has to be emptied of our bits of death.

IV

The difficult slow ease of scything hay —
It is comparable
To her adroitness with its wheels and flex.

V

After many days of toothache
To be grateful for the amnesia
Of a dentist's chair.

And after the long chaos of builders,
Carpenters, electricians,
Destroyers of plaster —

To be sensuously grateful
For the din of a hoover.

VI

In their iron age
The antique hoovers
— All pistons and steel tubes and levers —
In our square-carpeted drawing-rooms
Did not disguise their alienation.

I once turned a corner in Liverpool
And saw, disappearing down a side-street,
A vast, black-leaded steam locomotive,
O-four-O, colossal amid cars.

The antique hoovers, one felt,
Were de-railed like that.

VII

Hoovers would like to be precise.
Their robot souls yearn for clearances
Plus or minus a thousandth of an inch.
Always, by wobble or pile or buffer,
They are betrayed. Your average yard-brush
Is more of a precision instrument!

VIII

The soul of a hoover —
Is it the empty bag
That nothingness blows out like a sail?
Or is it the paradoxical geometry
Of the twisting belt, that burns
Sourly at the ingestion of a tack?

IX

There is a sub-culture of hoovers.
Hoovermen with wiry, terrier moustaches
Poke their heads from dusty limousines
To stop you in the road —

"That new belt I put in —
Has it remedied the fault?
Shall I come to see it?"

Their deft enquiries
Have strict authority over your thoughts.
They carry a king's seal, dispense his justice.

X

Its noise is more sensitive than you'd imagine.
It marks the difference between dusts.

XI

Most of us in a lifetime get to know
One, two, three hoovers. And that is enough.
We think we know the species.

But what of the professionals, the home-helps,
The Rent-a-maids from Hampstead?
Out of the hundreds of hoovers
Their fingers have caressed,

One, two, three stand out
Incomparable.

    As they think of these
Majestic, suave, blond super-hoovers,
Their thighs grow supple with pride,
Their pupils take on the steady gleam
Of an enthusiast, they are fulfilled.

We don't know the half of what hoovers can do.

XII

On what authority you say it I don't know,
But you say, "The hoover has no Muse".
Yet from the murk and ashes of our common
Existence, the accumulating death
Of our lives together in this room,
The hoover creates darkness, order, love.
Its wake in the waves of a carpet
Makes lines of growth, furrows a field like a plough.

Could Erato of the laughing eyes, Urania,
Or Melpomene who bore to a slinky river-god
The enticing Sirens, half-girl, half-duck —

Could these *echt*-Muses have ordered it better?

XIII

It's a great virtue in hoovers
You can switch them off.

WAYNE BURROWS

Biology Lessons

. . . no excellent beauty that hath not
some strangeness in the proportion.
    Francis Bacon

Here is the pathos of a stuffed monkey,
A jar of eyes from a child's bad dream,
A white rat flayed on a board with chrome
Pins, a thick, fruiting pungency on the air.
A child unlocks a skull, keeping count
Of each bone removed, while others admire
The cells of an inner cheek, or endure
The dissection of a freshly caught hare.

A girl wanders a line of shelves crammed
With bottles;*foetus, heart, larynx, tongue*;
Her eyes careful, her hand on the clock
Beating under her breast, and in her throat,
And the frail, rustling tug of her breath . . .
A recent hysterectomy contributes a cup
Of flesh, turning slowly in a womb of glass
That bears the inverted room like a lens.

Later, in a pure silence, sunlight streams
Through the still, green water of a tank
Where tadpoles turn from commas to frogs.
And here is a stirring near the Wormery —
Murky cortex, unwinding in a shaft of dust,
Its jar a sundial, a wand of rippling light
Cast between compassed initials, luminous
As an Aztec skull, a handful of fused quartz.

HILARY LLEWELLYN-WILLIAMS

If You Should Come To My House

If you should come to my house
warm with walking in the cold dusk
of the afternoon, walking quickly
being far too impatient to catch the bus,
to arrive at last all windswept at my door
with your white breath about you, if
you should knock suddenly
while I was making coffee just for
one, or cleaning out my cluttered room
in readiness for a chance visitor like you,
I'd run to meet you down every stair;
I'd fling my door wide to you, and soon
you would be sitting here
with my coffee in your hands, the whole place
in a muddle, but music on, and you'd feel
the fire's warmth on your face;
just supposing that you should come
out of the blowing leaves and autumn smoke
bright copper in the dropping sun, out
of the wind to my house and to my room
I would never turn you out into the rain:
I would greet you with a smile and take your coat
happy to sit you in my one chair,
and never shut my eyes to you again.

JOHN BARNIE

Lime Tree

It hummed like a power house,
I couldn't see why, and then,
Bees floating and hovering
Among green cumuli

That were piled high
With flowers, where they shuttled,
Attracted or repelled
By a powerful magnet.

If I touched that trunk
I might flash with a shout
Into cinder. Bees were components
In the tree's turbine,

Power building up
Through the evening, but earthed,
Unlikely to explode.
I stood drenched in scent.

Bees shipped nectar,
Stuffed pouches, bags,
Drifted in an electric hum,
Neutral to the charge.

Piratical, dark winged,
Swifts eddied, risked shock,
As bolts of black energy
Were flung from the tree.

CATHERINE FISHER

Severn Bore

Somewhere out there the sea has shrugged its shoulders.
Grey-green masses slip, rise, gather
to a ripple and a wave, purposeful, arrowing up
arteries of the land. Brown and sinuous, supple
as an otter, nosing upstream under the arching
bridge, past Chepstow, Lydney, Berkeley where a king
screamed; Westbury, where the old men
click stopwatches with grins of satisfaction;
slopping into the wellingtons of watchers,
swamping the nests of coots, splashing binoculars.
And so to Minsterworth meadows where Ivor Gurney's ghost
walks in sunlight, unforgotten; past lost
lanes, cow-trodden banks, nudging the reeds,
lifting the lank waterweed,
flooding pills, backwaters, bobbing the floats
of fishermen, the undersides of leaves and boats,
and gliding, gliding, over Cotswold's flawed
reflection, the sun swelling, the blue sky scored
with ripples, fish and dragonfly, stirred
by the drip and cloop of oars; and finally, unheard,
washing into the backstreets of the town to lie
at the foot of the high
cathedral, prostrate, breathless,
pilgrim from a far place;
refugee
from the ominous petulance of the sea.

ROBERT MINHINNICK

The Looters

The helicopter cameras
Bring us the freeze frames.
A black sea outlines each peninsula
As snow finer than marble dust
Blurs the steeples of the spruce.
Bad weather, the wisdom goes,
Brings a community together.
Tonight the screen is a mirror
And the news is us.

At a house in Bedlinog
A drift has left its stain
Like a river in flood
Against the highest eaves.
There will be a plaque placed there soon
As if for some famous son,
While the cataract at Cwm Nash
Is a thirty foot long stalactite
Full of eyes and mouths
And the dazzling short-circuits
Of a pillar of mercury.
An icicle uncirclable by three men.

Abandoned on the motorway
The container lorries are dislocated
Vertebrae. The freeze has broken
The back of our commerce
While on the farms, the snow-sieged
Estates, people return
To old technologies.

Meat is hung in double rows,
The carcasses identified
By the slashing beams.
Each one looms hugely,
Puzzling as a chrysalis
Under its silver condom of frost.
They sway like garments on a rack
When padlocks break and the freezer-
Doors swing out. It is too cold
Here to trail blood, where bread
Is frozen into breeze-blocks
And ten thousand tubes of lager
Sparkle under their ripping caul.
As flashlights zigzag up the wall
Tights turn red and tropical bronze
In each thin wallet.

The stranded drivers sleep in schools,
Their groups determined to uphold
The constitution of the snow.
Families smile through thermos steam,
A child with her kitten, blue
As a cinder, sucking a blanket:
The usual cast of winter's news,
As the commentary runs its snowplough
Through the annihilating white.

Outside the cars are scoops
of cumulus, and toboggans
Polish gutters in the drifts.
We never see the looters.
They move somewhere in the darkness
Through the blizzard, beyond the thin
Bright crescent of the screen,
Those people who have understood the weather
And make tomorrow's news.

GRAHAM THOMAS

Geography

You have come with your new geography
To test me out. The skin of your brow
Cradles the lost canals of Mars,
Is a maze of mediaeval fields,
Small hedges, tree-roots, contoured lines,
An atlas where I turn and turn
The pages endlessly.
          Now you are watching me
With particular care. I am a spider
Upside-down on the ceiling, a colour
Flapping on the line outside. Do you
See me any way but this? Or am I
The landscape where you first discover
Lines of darkness as the valleys fold,
The cusp beneath the eye, a trace
Of darkness there? Bored with watching,
You turn to someone else, a different smile,
And offer your calm, unshadowed face.

FRANCES WILLIAMS

Siesta Time

The sun stares at this place
Through the eye of a lens,
As if to set the grass on fire
In its orange light.
Dogs sleep on doorsteps
Like well-worn mats,
Breathing hotly through
Their wide nostrils.
Even the shadows hide by

Slowly recoiling into themselves
As cicadas buzz in the trees,
A bloodless pulsating in their
Tinder-dry husks.
Ants, like black beads,
Trickle down their holes
And green grapes sweat
In their close clusters.
Everyone sleeps until the light lengthens
And out of a shuttered window
A fat woman flaps her dusters.

JACI STEPHEN

For My Father

He always liked to start the day alone.
I heard the front door gently touch
My dream, and he was gone.
I caught the remnants of his routine at dawn:
His cup thick with sugar, the pot still warm.

I remember he used to brush sand
From my feet; sit me on a wall at the beach.
His fingers probed between my toes,
He rolled my socks over my feet
And buckled my shoes on the middle notch.

It was his cool hand I felt
Against my forehead when I was sick:
He cradled my skull over lavatory bowls
And buckets; carried me back to bed,
Turned my pillows and plumped them cold.

211

I am easier in his silence,
Finding him suddenly like an afterthought;
Too much love to want reminding of,
A constant pain that is the father in my blood,
An itch, like sand, rubbing between the toes.

CHRISTOPHER MILLS

Never Forget Yuh Kaairdiff

"Kaairdiff is well known to be the world's most boring crapital
city."
                    Eggon Istie 'Welsh Tourist Baard'.

Frank Fanakapan's on d'mitch
inis bestest daps
onis fastest underang bogey
like a proper Beano comic

Mad Motter donkeyin
racing froo Grange-end gard'ns
causin a whoppin great malarky
dodgin d' diddykoys

scramblin cross d'daffs
crackin jelly froo d' chewlips
an d' Parky's frowin a wobbly
totally outta d' window like

"BLOODY LIDDLE DOZZO'S" he yells
all jottled up to is nodgem
"YOO'LL GET SUM GROLLOP
YOO EVER PARK YUR ARSE ROUND YUR AGEN"

Motter might be be-jobbled
but Fanakapan, ee's norra dill

iss is dream, when ee grows up
t'be obbledihoy t'd' queen

An'd Parky's ad a majorum
is germodgems gone all manky
"farawackin bollawocks" ee baas
"I'm off down d'skinouse"

aark aark d'laark
frum Kaairdiff Aarms Paark
I'll aave a Claarksie pie
an an aaf an aaf a Daark
aan
a banaana jam saanwidge!

STEWART BROWN

From: Splashes From The Cauldron

Quickening

The old wives said, when they felt
that first faint butterfly in the womb
it was the foetus come alive, becoming *quick*
as if before that act of wilfulness,
that first turning over in the crumpled bed
of flesh, the child was *not,* was just
a superior form of grit in a superior oyster,
wombstone, too often tombstone, the Spirit
might bless pearl. We scoff at such simplicities.

Today your mother said she felt you stir.
I go to find your cot up in the attic,
begin to paint your room, she sorts out clothes
and flicks through pages in *The Book of Names*
our preparations quickening, the tests confirmed.

"Mummy's got a baby in her tummy . . ."
"Did she eat it?"

CannibMum, stirring her cooking pot
of infant stew, bang-belly-calabash
breasts like uglifruit, grunts Afro-Celtic
curses as she stomps the firelight.
She is an awesome sight, a body quite
possessed, replete with mysteries
that creak and gurgle and burn and weep.

Her shadow is a bulbous baobab,
the witches' tree: squat, hollow, the gateway
to infinity, a chapel where the spirits
pass from one world to the next. She is taboo,
holy, a sacred shrine men worship at
but may not enter. Her priestesses death's
midwives, delivering souls into new life.

BRYAN ASPDEN

Doctor's Papers

To misquote a long ago friend, ideas among poets are like fleas on a dog. Useless in themselves, they prevent us from falling into a torpor.

The ideas that got these words to their feet come in two recent announcements on how to write poetry. The first is Greg Hill's editorial to *Anglo Welsh Review* No. 82, which separates sheep from goats by quoting Geoffrey Hill's distinction between writers who deal with "dark disputed matter" and those who merely "push on pragmatically with the matter in hand". The second is John Barnie's essay in *Planet* no. 57, which cautions us to avoid politics and write only under the influence of creative urges.

I have written this article to counter these editorial warnings —
spoiling their views by rough handling and taking them further
than they meant to go, deliberately, in the hope of sparking a
dialectic.

Greg Hill's editorial is brief, but to several points. Dark
disputers are concerned with language and content, with
relationship between form and meaning. They think deeply and
look for universal understanding of their place and time. The
quieter virtues are easily prodded from the world's eye by
pragmatic pushers. Pushers don't waste time with linguistic
problems. They're clever, fluent. Their easy command of words
hides their essential frivolity. They posture. They use empty
rhetoric. But they won't last. Made sterile by self-titillation, their
seed can't get past its own space and time.

To test these coins I rummaged for the darkest words from the
darkest work I could remember, and surfaced with:

> Good things of day begin to droop and drowse,
> While night's black agents to their prey do rouse.

From *Macbeth,* and then disputatious *Coriolanus:*

> forget not
> With what contempt he wore the humble weed,
> How in his suit he scorned you:

Murky enough for either Hill, but what got them to the point was
the threat of tyranny in James VI's accession to the throne, and
the need for a jab at the cockatoo Raleigh. It's because they were
sharpened in real quarrels that the words cut at our own perches
and thrones.

Ben Jonson, a nimble-spirited catso who had the leigerity and
the whiggies and the daggers in the nose, lacked the confluction of
powers to frame a brimstone tragedy. But what of it? His classical
Catiline and *Sejanus* have faded because he failed to fit them into
his own times, but his comedies of London street life still buzz.

Catfooting through the Cannon Street Hotel and emerging
under the brown fog of a winter dawn, Eliot's darkness is not in
dispute. But Joyce, parodying everyone in sight, tapping a

French novelist for his stream of consciousness, hijacking Homer and mixing his Anglo-Irish epic from Dublin Hop Bitters, was the arch pragmatist. His declaration of independence turned Eliot's Celtic mythology to "a night, late, long time agone, in an auldstance eld" and "the blarniest blather in all Corneywall."

Even Yeats left Oisin and Cuchulain for "that raving slut who keeps the till"; his gong-tormented sea for "the foul rag and bone shop of the heart."

Is this Hill's argument? Street sweepings aren't poetry? Or are only poetry if they're Yeats? It isn't easy to tell. He uses logic with a *trompe l'oeil* panache reminiscent of surrealist painting. When he writes "merely" outside quotation marks, and "pragmatist" inside them, whose "merely" is it? Greg's or Geoffrey's? Or both Hills'? Whichever way, well fudged, sir. For we are in a court where presumption is stronger than evidence and where tone is all. The praise sounds as though it has been delivered from a podium. The invective, though intemperate, is fluffy, as though the author of "an upstart crow, beautified with our feathers" had sold out to the Jaeger Knitting Company.

Writers are not mentioned in the case against them. We have to guess who is accused of having sunk to "trivial amusement" and "intellectual titillation". Could that tyke from Barnsley with the dormobile roadshow, who ends his performance with a little dance and a "thank you, thank you" be one of them? Or the Faber cocoa maker who turned the Waste Land into limericks and does frivolous takeoffs of Ted Hughes? The retired copywriter who coined 'Strongbow Cider' and now churns out acid epigrams of indecent shortness on the contemporary scene? Our own selfconfessed cad who wrote "casual passion is rather confusing" and "I was Welsh and got her pregnant"?

Hill names no names, but he gives a clue. While he would rather have people who think more deeply, satirists, he suggests, could possibly be let in. Pope, Dryden, Swift, Molière and Orwell would probably make it. Waugh (E.), Wilde and Wendy Cope might not. Other cardsharpers playing the riverboats of literature, and also in need of positive vetting, could be political propagandists and journalists disguised as poets, who are seen in their company.

It's an awkward situation, and I can understand Hill's confusion. Who are these people who prefer reason to imagination, wit to emotion? They can't be accused of lack of concern with language. They translated the *Iliad* and the *Aeneid* for practice. But they don't fit the Romantic notion of poetry as a branch of aviation. One modern writer, convinced that Pope was a true poet and not just a clever student who wrote his essays in heroic couplets, looked for a sign. He found it at last. Pope wrote in a ruined tower, at midnight, surrounded by owls and bats.

But what gives most umbrage is Hill's plugging of universal as somewhere we should try and get used to. This is balloonman's sales talk — those rinsed tomorrows, those pale blue other-wheres . . .

I prefer Walt Whitman's:

> I heard what was said of the Universe.
> It is middling well as far as it goes — but is that all?

William Carlos Williams believed "the only universal is local."

> and a white birch
> with yellow leaves
> and few
> and loosely hung
>
> and a young dog
> jumped out
> of the old barrel.

It's the immediate, the moment, the connecting with now, that's the window to this reality.

John Barnie is easier to come at: he tells us what he's writing about. His argument is that poets aren't self-propelled but must wait for inspiration to press the starter. They can't be expected to respond just like that to political events, and anyone who asks them to try is showing his ignorance. He concludes the "political verse of any persuasion that has survived as art would make a very slim volume."

After reading this I had another look at *The Faber Book of Political Verse*, edited by Tom Paulin. It's 482 pages long.

My counter-arguments are:

That the separation between art and politics, between religion and politics and education and politics, is an assumption made by the state in its own interest and we wear it because it's comfortable.

That poetry is not more inspired than the Tour de France.

Once there was the Muse and when she went to a happier land she left all that she had to her two daughters, imagination and inspiration. Imagination was adopted by a solid bourgeois family and is doing well. Inspiration, after a series of stormy affairs, drowned in the Bay of Naples but appears to her admirers in spiritual lookalikes. Barnie knows one of these. She is an "uncertain" power, revealing herself in "unexpected surges of creativity". To poets, that is. It is fairly clear she does not visit novelists.

He says that poets, unlike novelists, can't just go to their study and write. If they try, they suffer "head-scratching, window-gazing, wandering thoughts, idle pulling of books from the shelf." Will-power and regular hours being out, they have to rely instead on "sudden irrational fits". Dickens or Faulkner, Barnie explains, could not possibly have worked this way. Neither could Wordsworth, Milton, Spenser, Dante, Chaucer, Langland, Virgil or Homer. Or R.S. Thomas: "My first job is to get to my study and to set myself in motion and set myself to work. You can't just hang about waiting for inspiration." Seamus Heaney believes poems have to be "dug up", and reminds us that Yeats wrote "we must labour to be beautiful."

Poems, for Barnie, come unforseen "often written at speed in quite complex forms", their final shape "essentially there" barring "minor adjustments and polishing". Well yes, comets fall and change our lives. But they don't run them. R.S. Thomas writes "the idea of words flowing ready mixed is a fiction. Most poets compose with great difficulty, choosing and rejecting and altering their words, until often the finished draft bears little relation to what they begin with." Dylan Thomas wrote many of his first versions while still at school and spent his life reshaping them for his *Collected Poems*. Yeats's first drafts were damp twigs to be coaxed into reluctant fire. Ted Hughes has advocated writing to a set theme with a time limit, to create a crisis in the mind and unlock imagination. Basil Bunting drew a diagram of 'Brigg Flats' before he wrote it. The organisation man is part of our make-up.

218

So is the competitor. We share with athletes the energy that can be summoned after long effort in response to a challenge. Milton, in one of those autobiographical asides that help us through 'Paradise Lost', rehearses the process of inducing vision:

> all mist from thence
> Purge and disperse, that I may see and tell
> Of things invisible to mortal sight.

Barnie's idea of poets as divinely gifted amateurs has one advantage. It reduces the strain on us and leaves the slog to novelists, film makers, musicians, playwrights, painters: people who do their five finger exercises.

In campaigning to keep poetry clean, he warns us to beware of political activists, who will try to put pressure on us. His example of pressure is interesting. He means a speech by Kim Howells at a writer's conference. Kim Howells "berated" writers for not producing great art from the miner's strike. I think Barnie should have paused before answering that political poetry can't be done, and if it can it's a freak accident, and if it isn't an accident it's so rare it doesn't count. Kim Howells may not know what he's talking about, but he might have read Idris Davies's *Angry Summer*.

The question is, why can't we do it now? Barnie is right to point to a failure of language, wrong in his diagnosis of the failure. He says that politicians use rhetoric, like Cicero, though they're not so good at it. Their metaphors are clothes pegged to language. Poets' metaphors are the real thing, with a "mysterious atavistic quality". Is he quite sure that our poems are better than Cicero? What I notice about politicians isn't rhetoric. It's clichés paraded as discoveries. The way words slither like fish trying to get upstream without being caught. Raucous imprecision. The mushier the language, the more bullying the voice.

The reason, I believe, lies in our post-imperialist attitude to education, politics, culture, work and play, which we keep in separate rooms for fear that one will fall out of bed and wake the others up. Hence the outraged shushes when bishops talked about the miners' strike, or schools teach peace studies.

Raymond Williams in *The Long Revolution* describes how

culture and politics in our society have become estranged from each other. The separation has "led to a very damaging suppression of relationships. Each kind of activity suffers." We end up with uncultured politicians, and ineffectual culture: a closed circuit of arts, education as the protector of the status quo. This isn't natural growth. It has been made to meet the centralising needs of empire which require politicians to concentrate power in their own hands. More so than ever when the threads slip and they hold on with increasing virulence and brutality.

Barnie accepts this situation, as he accepts the language of politicians and poets the way they are. But why should we put up with either? Poets have minds to make up, as well as pennies from heaven, and there are more ways to travel than sitting in the waiting room.

It's a failure of Anglo-Welsh writing that when we turn to politics we leave poetry behind and wave banners of emotion and sincerity instead, as though damp gunpowder and rusty bullets don't matter if the cause is right. So much yeast produces so much soggy dough.

Barnie quotes Denise Levertov as an awful example of what goes wrong when poets "dedicate their art to the cause":

> Yes, it is as well that we have gathered
> in this chapel to remember
> the students shot at Kent State
>
> but let us be sure we know
> our gathering is a mockery unless
> we remember also
> the black students shot at Orangeburg two years ago . . .
>
> And I went on and said . . .

This fails, Barnie says, in spite of its "white hot indignation", because it isn't poetry but political prose.

I'd say it's neither politics nor prose. It's the drone of a Nimmo vicar who knows how to preach without waking the congregation. All prig and no poke. Compare Irina Ratushinskaya's recognition of the executioner:

My classmate said: "Good evening.
How unlucky you've been.
I've always believed in soft measures.
But somehow no-one asked me,
They just gave me a pistol and sent me.
I mean, I can't . . . anyway, it's no good . . .
There's nothing we can do to change things.
If they hadn't sent me, it'd have been another.
Perhaps somebody you didn't know.

Introducing the book this passage was taken from, Joseph Brodsky writes of "the state's fear and hatred of the genuine poet, its jealousy for that which will outlive it." No government department fears our poems. Why should they? We've traded effectiveness for a seat among the sublime. It's a consolation we don't deserve and would be better without.

When political pressure becomes more stringent it can't be escaped, and poetry finds resources to absorb it. I think of Rozewicz's life in occupied Poland: "odd menial jobs to keep alive, graduation from clandestine military school, participation in the Resistance, publication from a makeshift secret press . . .

I am twenty four
led to slaughter
I survived

Or Mandelstam's attack on Stalin — "the laughing cockroaches on his top lip" — and his house arrest:

You took away all the oceans and all the room.
You gave me my shoe size in earth with bars around it.
Where did it get you? Nowhere.
You left me my lips, and they shape words, even in silence.

And I think of Rimbaud, after the collapse of the Paris Commune and the massacre of its participants, trying to create revolution by liberating language and perception. Lorca, Alberti, Paz, Neruda, writing for a people, against suppression, their words weapons we can still turn against the fascist tide.

These voices are a long slog from Wales. They can be forgiven for not having infiltrated Barnie's essay. But Michael Longley,

Paul Muldoon, Tom Paulin, writing political poetry in Northern Ireland, in circumstances which reflect and involve our own? It must have been a job to keep them out, and let in 'Mum and the Sothsegger', 'The Hundred Years War' and Tennyson's 'Ode on the Death of The Duke of Wellington' instead. Even Yeats's poem on the Easter rising is nudged aside as the product of a mixed marriage between "external pressure" and "internal disturbance".

Barnie's drift is that political poetry, if it exists, doesn't have a political persuasion, isn't an act of will, and doesn't serve a political function. He brushes off what he calls "left wing" thirties poetry. But what of Auden's later response to Brezhnev's invasion of Czechosovakia:

> The ogre does what ogres can,
> Deeds quite impossible to man.
>
> But one prize escapes its reach:
> The ogre cannot master speech.
>
> Across a subjegated plain,
> Among its desolate and slain,
>
> The ogre strolls with hands on hips,
> While drivel gushes from his lips.

This is not atavistic. It could even be rhetoric. It is certainly political, partisan and poetry.

Or Muldoon's quizzical but engaged comments on 'The Boundary Commission'. A shower of rain:

> Had stopped so cleanly across Golightly's lane
> It might have been a wall of glass
> That had toppled over. He stood there, for ages,
> To wonder which side, if any, he should be on.

Enzensberger writes that unless we feel the sweat of history we are nothing. Barnie's essay has the fluttery feeling of having come unstuck from history. His recoil from events is clearest when he describes a work as "reportage, not poetry", as though Louis

MacNeice had never written 'Autumn Journal'.

Does this matter? Why should Barnie, or anyone else, write political poetry or see how it can be written, if they don't want to? No reason, perhaps. Only his list of explanations for not doing so reads like a claim for disability benefit; and "the world's great rage" may not leave us alone much longer. Doctor's papers are a doddle not a cure.

IRENE THOMAS

From: Floral Tribute — Ebbw Vale, 1987

News Of A Garden Festival!

"Read all about it"
in *Argus* and *Echo* and *Gwent Gazette*.
Obituaries take second place,
the interest is in flowers.
They will mask the grave
in a plot to re-cover Victoria
and bring back colour,
with blossoms blown flame and red,
but with a sweeter scent.

Cwm and Waunlwyd stir in their sleep.
Smile over the dream, and slump down again.
Victoria as yet unmoved,
waits for people to walk over the grave.

Up Ebbw,
the Council celebrate and drink champagne,
getting up noses.
There will be swings and roundabouts,
as they build castles, with people up in air.

And in the gardens,
will there be rooting in fertile soil,
places for the wall-flowers,
forget-me-nots and red-hot pokers?

And when the visitors have gone
will flowers burn in bitter wind,
wither in the blasting?
They will need stems as wiry as the heather
on Myndydd Carn-y-Cefn,
blooms like clenched fists,
bunched against blows,
from the hunched shoulders of the mountains.

Bill Evans stands on his allotment,
above the desolation of the burial ground
brittle underfoot with burned-out cinders
from Becker and Open Hearth.
Watches grey rain lash the flat lifeless waste,
leaving liquid coal-dust
pooled round rusting trucks on the South Inlet sidings.
Tries to imagine an oriental garden.

Shakes his head and gets to work,
cleaning up unwanted cuttings,
ties and remains of young sprouts
clinging to old stems.

Waits for green shoots.

VUYELWA CARLIN

The Cellar

— No, there were no dust-suits once —
People walked out, even so;
They could run — I told you
What that means — the wind,

The sunlight — gold —
Touched them, and no harm done.

— The houses were overground,
Full of air — it could make you drunk
Just to think! — there was green
And blue; and huge

Huge basins of water
That glittered and jumped.

— The rain kept them multitudinous —
You could gulp its pearly douse,
Clean as old icebergs,
Soft as tears. —

The young alabaster-brows
Flopped obedient, all ears.

SALLY ROBERTS JONES

Provincial?

The bus, as always, is late.
We sit, congenial strangers, in a row
Under a cast-iron roof by the School of Art.
Above us the grey church looms,

An abandoned cathedral; nearby, on the tidy grass,
Five flaking stones box in the forgotten career
Of Sir William Nott, who once, in the distant Indies,
Was master of life and death.

The town, as always, is busy.
Insistent cars
Nudge in their flocks through the streets,
While prosperous farmers
Chaffer around the pens in their shabby raincoats.
In the church lies Sir Richard Steele,
Washed up by a swell of loving
On this green, provincial shore —
Whale in our lake of minnows.

Prosperous always; where only the echoes of anger
Disturb the neat walls.
Here nothing's begun; the world is a stir of reflections
On glass in the sun.

The church clock has stopped.
Below, in the shadowy silence, Sir Rhys is entombed
In the usual crumbling grandeur; without whom
Spaniards might rule in New York, or India
Stir in a Mongol dream:
Without whom Hamlet is uncreated — and the world
Spins on a different pivot to its end?

JOHN GURNEY

The Swift

Something was recovered, suddenly.
The weather had developed, and the wind
had fanned its wings, and driven on the rain
that poured down without pause, as night and day,
it washed away the insects from the air,

thus weakening the swifts. Overtired,
unable to avoid the northern air,
to skim beyond the outskirts of the storm
outwitting its dark thunders, gliding past
its blue down-burning lightnings, all the swifts
flew lower in the evening, clutched our walls
to hang like stencilled shadows. One alone
had fallen to our doorstep, where it lay,
immobile, stretched, just breathing, with its head
set quietly on the leather of your shoe
as if it felt the heat, the human warmth
that flowed out from your body. You had stopped.
You stared down at the bird in disbelief.
Its dark brown wings were stiff as scimitars
and wider than a kestrel's, glimmering
in glassy dark translucence as it kept
one eye unclosed, the other flickering
beneath its shutting lid, as if it held
its consciousness half-open. Now at last
its movements had been stilled, its restlessness,
that scribbled, mad agraphia of its flight,
scarce seen, but gone away, a vanishing,
as fleeting as the quality of time,
a quivering of meaning. And its calls
that peeted down the street, between the trees
like whistles blown at spirits, or the sounds
of scrying-stones transfigured by the wind
were silenced, as submissively he stretched
where yesterday the nestlings had been dropped
unfledged, and bald, half-naked. Then you bent,
lifted him, and set him to your breast,
held him in the warm skin of your palms
as if cupped in a nest, his tight beak shut,
unwilling then to open, as you shared
the silence of his blissful timelessness
in absolute absorption, rested in
the certainty of presence, suddenly
at one, and self-sufficient. But he moved:
grasped you with his sharply needled claws,

re-opened then the great gape of his throat,
the wide yawn made for grazing at the flies
that glittered in the meadows of the air,
unclosing then the black balls of his eyes
that scanned you like a hawk, a predator,
alive again, desiring. So you knelt:
took him to the window, to the grass,
the movement of the breeze, the swaying boughs
that pricked him into action, as he moved,
flashed with an activity of wings
that took off in a straight low-level flight
that banked then through the garden, cleared the wall,
rose up past the black roof of the barn
to climb off through the evening, flittering
a last shade in the twilight. And at night,
alone now in the stillness of the room,
you stare up at the glass waste of the stars
imagining activity, your eyes
still searching for a movement, for a glide,
a body like an arrow in a bow
that sleeps upon the wing, some two miles high,
alive there with the young unmated males
untroubled by the dark shade of the earth,
illumined by the full face of the moon.

LUCIEN JENKINS

Welch

1.

Let us take our history
fold it and tuck it in our wallet
like money

take the place itself
and hang it round our necks
like a charm.

Shall we examine the slate,
leaf through it for alibis?

Let us speak rather loudly about beer
and hills as though it were clever
and make much of the word waelisc.

2.

Foreigned, my mouth plugged with English
like a too-big tongue half choking me
as you and your family giggled and bickered in Welsh,
I pulled on my boots and went into the rain.

Cymraeg, I muttered, going past the pigs,
down to the sea, the corgi podging through the mud.
Saesneg: a mean, snap-jawed word
like a toad catching a fly with its tongue might say.
Saesneg!
While all the time my boots
mouthed in the soft-lipped mud:
Welch. Welch. Welch.

TONY CURTIS

Couples From The Fifties

Vague shapes stiff and grey all those miles away
The Coronation in our front-room — dull monotype, limited
    edition.

★

I smelt the Alvis's leather back seat as my father's radio declared
War on Egypt — the Suez route to India, East of Anthony Eden.

★

Mau Mau, Eoka, National Service, Singapore, Berlin.
The war won, the Empire dimming, the curtains coming down.

★

Rock 'n' Roll came to Carmarthen, two years late — the
    usherettes
Amazed as kids jived in the *Lyric's* aisles, just like the *Pathé
    News.*

★

Buddy, Elvis, Cliff, Gene, the original Comets and Bill.
The sweetest love-song ya ever heard — Don and Phil.

★

The outcasts, the lunch-time loners, the misunderstood,
We trekked to the lost geyser springs of Fecci's espresso.

★

Coffee steam blends with Woodbine smoke and through it all
The Mekon Juke-box doing slow-motion card tricks.

★

In Blackpool I held my autograph book for David Nixon — in
    colour!
Who made cards machine-gun, vanish, then float back into view
    like gulls.

★

Dad's challenge — up the Lynton hill in the little black Austin,
    first gear:
Then down on the brake to what the sea had left of the sea-wall,
    Lynmouth.

★

In the grey-dark matinees of the *Lyric* I plundered
The idea of oysters in a coral reef of petticoats.

PETER GRUFFYDD

Colonial Kind

These who occupy Portmeirion beach
are not a Raj, the curry and whiskey
sort who used Celtic mercenaries,
Gurkhas, anyone willing or pressed
to hand, to quarter an empire,
barking for chota-peg, punkah-wallah.
These bawl at their dogs which tank
through picnics, erratically
shower sand over homeric craps
then steam around, anarchic,
propelled by their owners' empiric
angst, while the ladies, doling out
sandwiches, dropped vests, lost spades,
are again the backbone of it all.

Genteel effusions of Italianate
pomp (*Il Duce* would have felt at home)
surround a group sucking ices
dolefully: Yud think dey wooden
bother with'er Welsh signs, eyh?
No, bloody stewpid. Ah mean, we're all
English 'ere, arn'we? Cept forrer Krauts . . .
Course. Anner bloody Frog's an' Dutch.

Course, yes. Yuh'cn easy reckenize
'em; all got lotsa camras, arn'ey!
Ah. Oh-ah . . . bloody soft! Ah.

Every tyrant fears each citizen
is ruler, steward and base lord,
knows their statues stand forgotten,
reason gone with the weather's hand
into greyer yesterdays.

What is the unease I feel,
stumbling on the softer sands
on which all empires, aspirant
or just defunct, are built,
and wandering on the sand-bar,
a boomerang sweep of mountains
careening ponderously round the bay?
Aber Iâ, the older name,
is eaten up with tourist dreams,
Portmeirion with tomorrow's lords.

PETER FINCH

Severn Estuary ABC

A is a hat. Sun on my head.
B binoculars I'm using
C across the water. Largest concentration.
D is design. Planned.
E in Europe. Believe that.
F is mud flats, wading birds
G for godwit, green sandpiper, grey plover.
H is heavy population, heavy water.
I'm informed. I watch tv. My hat is
Just there to stop the sun burning.
Know what does it?
L is little suns in bottles. Heat.

M is the mighty atom.
N for no trouble in Oldbury, Hinkley Point, Berkley.
Old stuff, I know. They're not sure.
P soup of a public explanation.
Quantity before quality. The fuel of the future.
R is rich someone's salting somewhere. There's always someone.
Severn seeped solid. Sold down the river.
T is truth. Piece of fiction.
Ah yes.
U is understanding. It's safe.
V is very safe. Formation of ducks. Skinhead. Thatcher.
We buy it.
X marks the spot. The insidious ingress. The cancer.
Why don't we do something?
Z is the sound of us listening.

MICHAEL LONGLEY

Detour

I want my funeral to include this detour
Down the single street of a small market town,
On either side of the procession such names
As Philbin, O'Malley, MacNamara, Keane.
A reverent pause to let a herd of milkers pass
Will bring me face to face with grubby parsnips,
Cauliflowers that glitter after a sunshower,
Then hay rakes, broom handles, gas cylinders.
Reflected in the slow sequence of shop windows
I shall be part of the action when his wife
Draining the potatoes into a steamy sink
Calls to the butcher to get ready for dinner
And the publican descends to change a barrel.
From behind the one locked door for miles around
I shall prolong a detailed conversation
With the man in the concrete telephone kiosk
About where my funeral might be going next.

PAUL GROVES

At The Church Of St. Mary The Virgin

What discomfited was that each
was a glaring grinner
who would sink poisoned fangs
into you as into a peach
or a plate of merangues
served after dinner.

What scared was their lack
of compunction, the way
they pitchforked the damned with impunity,
deaf to entreaty. Rack,
tongs with flaming embers, flay-
ing knives: there was no immunity

once you were dead. This window's
lurid mosaic proved
that at any second the unwary
could slip. Sin goes
before you constantly.
And what of that God who loved

and forgave? No sign of him here.
Demerit writ large this was, a hell
of coloured fragments. Even one eye,
loose in its socket, could engender fear
which would last all week. The sombre bell
reminded the child that it must die

and face the upshot of every mistake.
I hid behind Mummy. She would protect
forever, I thought, but each demon knew
she was glass and would break
into a kaleidoscope of tears. I drew
close to her skirts, composure wrecked,

and she cupped her hands around
my head. Choice was delayed:
I could play in the sun and laugh
at shadows. But then the ground
opened, and she entered its shade,
and cut me in half.

OLIVER REYNOLDS
City

What makes the city possible
is rain
In the snug
the palate surges
and talk is artesian
Brooks moon
past the bomb factory
Rain-fatted streams
deepen to a Frisian brown
and push to the sea
persistent as myth
The artificial lake rises
around its mock lighthouse
commemorating
an arctic explorer
who never returned

Two princes in the tower
trying to escape
hand in hand from history
we'd found all the doors locked
When we returned shamefaced
the bull-headed guide
waved her keys at us
and then continued
her labyrinthine patter
As the tour moved on
we lingered by the bath
made for the Marquis
from a sarcophagus with me

holding your hair
like a clew

The night-workers
at the mail-order warehouse
sort the last lorry-load
before the meal break
In the locker-room
they sit without talking
finish their tea and sandwiches
and then fold and unfold
their newspapers
When they return to work
the regular owl has ghosted in
to perch among the roof-struts
pebble-eyed and silent

The night-workers finish
between four and five
and leave singly
crossing the dark city
with the wet roads to themselves
Car radios are tuned to music
or a sports commentary
beamed from the antipodes
Someone on a bike
climbing a hill
snuggles into the wake
of the first milk float

We climbed the castle keep
above the airy city
spread like a gift
and the strip of sea
with its flat island
and steep island
You had new boots
and I gave you tissues
to fold around your heels
Undressed for bed
your feet would be blooded
by two raw holes
domestic stigmata
I'd put my fingers to

Brick by brick
day by day
the old city
is becoming
the new city
The brewery's new chimney
gleams like a missile

Hops have lost
their public smell
the half-pall half-tang
that hung over town
The castle walls mix stone
Norman on Roman
We speak from the rubble
of the old tongues
The late-night buses
wait in the bays
engines running
Privatised colours
waver in a glare
of sodium and alcohol
The radio-controller
counts the minutes to eleven
Released on the hour
the ponderous shoal
shivers into movement

DAVID LLOYD

The Margin And The Center In Contemporary American Poetry

With hundreds of literary magazines churning out thousands of poems and a burgeoning book publishing industry of university presses, small presses and trade houses releasing hundreds of anthologies and poetry collections each year, any attempt to follow contemporary American poetry in a comprehensive way becomes an immense and disheartening task.[1] Readers and critics might decide to follow the work of poets, presses or magazines in a given region; but when New York State alone is home to almost 500 'little' magazines and presses,[2] even narrowing one's focus regionally cannot solve the problem. Despite the tremendous literary output, American poets have a sense of living and working, as Robert Dana puts it, "in a country that is genuinely indifferent to poetry".[3] Poets are not sure that their output reaches a significant audience; and they certainly are not assured of reviews in either newspapers or large-circulation periodicals. Rather than trying to address all these facets of contemporary poetry or comment on all poets who have achieved some status or fame, a more realistic approach might be to isolate the direction or development most likely to shape contemporary poetry of the 1990's.

I would like to set a context for discussing what I think is the most significant development in recent American poetry by taking a glance at earlier decades, when literary output was less frenetic. The 1950's in the United States saw the ascendency of 'academic' poetry, propounding a rational and intellectual poetics influenced by the New Criticism and indebted to the writings of T.S. Eliot, whose reputation as a poet and critic was at its peak. Like 'the Movement' and 'the Group' in England, American academic verse was not socially-oriented and not overtly political — I say 'not overtly' since the very absence of obtrusive polemics in the poetry dominating what Robert Lowell calls "the tranquilized Fifties" betrays a political stance supportive of the status quo, a desire to see poetry more as a passive "superior amusement" than as an active "mode of resistance".[4]

Academic poetry *was* American poetry in the 1950's, at least as far as the general readership and the established critics were concerned. But during these years another poetry developed which was antagonistic to the mainstream publishing of the Eisenhower years: 'Beat' poetry — the poetry of the San Francisco Renaissance, written by Gregory Corso, Allen Ginsberg, Gary Snyder and others. Associated with jazz music, socialist or anarchist politics, and the burgeoning drug culture, and opposing the dominant ethos of materialist and capitalist American culture,[5] the Beats had to fight for recognition and publication, at least until Lawrence Ferlinghetti established City Lights Books. The obscenity trial following the publication of Ginsberg's *Howl* in 1956 is the most famous attempt to suppress this radical voice in American poetry, but the more successful and insidious method was simple ridicule and derision in the popular press.[6]

Ginsberg and Snyder, the best of the San Francisco

Renaissance poets, have moved from the margin to the center of American poetry in the 1970's and 80's. But in the 1950's their work — published not in the high circulation quarterlies but in (very) little magazines such as *Coyote's Journal* and by small presses such as City Lights Books — were so radical partly because they re-introduced politics and social awareness to American poetry in an overt manner.[7] That fact is one of their great achievements, although political poetry in the United States would be much more fully realised in the late 1960's and early 1970's.

In the 1960's and 70's a variety of 'schools' of poets developed in the United States, including the 'Confessionals" (e.g. Snodgrass, Plath, Sexton), the 'Deep Imagists' (e.g. Bly, Merwin), the 'Projectivists' (also called the 'Black Mountain Poets', e.g. Olson, Duncan, Creeley, Levertov), and the 'New York' school (O'Hara, Berrigan). None of these groups, however, clearly oriented their poetry outwards — towards the society the poets lived in, to criticise, analyse or celebrate its culture and history. But two dramatic developments of the 1960's — the Civil Rights movement and the accompanying race riots, and the Vietnam War — helped forge a shared political awareness for a number of poets while, ironically, deepening divisions already evident in American culture. The resulting politically-charged atmosphere, most apparent on the college campuses, caused poets to find their poetic visions, in Cary Nelson's words, to be "largely detached from a sense of immediate political reality".[8] In addressing that detachment, a number of poets radically revised their stance towards politics, the self and society. One-time Beat poet Leroi Jones, for instance, became the radicalised black poet and playwright Amiri Baraka. Adrienne Rich, whose early work showed the polished characteristics of 1950's academic poetry, became active in civil rights and anti-war campaigns, ultimately discovering a new voice and audience in a radical feminist poetics.

Some critics have argued that attention to the Vietnam War by America's best poets produced some very bad results. In *Enlarging the Temple*, his book on American poetry of the 1960's, Charles Altieri shows sympathy for the attempts of poets like Denise Levertov to escape the limits of what he terms the "immanentist mode of poetic thought" that develops "concrete moments in which the numinous emerges out of the quotidian".[9] Yet he believes that the poets of the 1960's were largely unable to reconcile their essentially apolitical, private poetics with the political, public imperative of racial turmoil and the Vietnam war. For Altieri, "Levertov's poetry during the years of war becomes for the most part increasingly strident, abstract, and verbally dead as she grapples with reconciling essentially personal modes of poetic awareness with her need for public moral structures".[10]

Some members of the generation that achieved prominence in the 1960's (such as Levertov, Snyder, Bly, and Ginsberg) continued into the next decade struggling with the formal difficulties inherent in writing poetry addressing public issues such as nuclear arms, neo-colonialist wars in El Salvador and Nicaragua, and the gulf between monied upperclasses and disenfranchised underclasses. But when the Vietnam War ended in American withdrawal, the Warren Court established new precedents for Civil Rights law, and the Nixon administration collapsed as a result of Watergate, poets drew back from exploring political and social material, returning once again to writing which explores self more than society.

Despite the continued political focus maintained by poets after the turbulent 1960's (the recent poetry of Hayden Carruth provides one example), the late 70's proved to be a transition to the 'new conservative agenda' of the 80's — the Reagan years. It is no coincidence that one of the developments in the 1980's poetry is 'new formalism', a loose grouping of poets and critics championing traditional forms in opposition to the 'open forms' (such as projective verse) of the 1960's. This harkening to the old poetic order coincides with the mainstream American reaction against 1960's anti-material openness — evident in the acceptance of supply-side economics ('Reaganomics') and the burgeoning consumer-oriented 'yuppie' generation. The conservative swing in higher education, articulated most recently by Allen Bloom's *The Closing of the American Mind*, provides another example of the same desire to return to a pre-1960's state of grace, as if the Vietnam War, the Civil Rights Movement and Watergate never occurred; or, in poetic terms, as if the breakthroughs in form and subject effected by poets of the late 1950's and 60's constitute an aberration rather than an advance.

Two critical commonplaces recur in most attempts to describe the tenor of 1980's American poetry. The first is the perception that most poetry originates in 'writing workshops': university programs which train young writers in fiction or poetry. The contention is that these programs churn out highly-crafted, polished but self-absorbed lyrics which display an irritating similarity of form. The second commonplace is that the irrelevance of contemporary American poetry is apparent in its tiny readership, and that what readership there is consists of poets or would-be poets who subscribe to magazines and buy books because they themselves publish or hope to publish. But I am not convinced that workshop writers are primarily responsible for the similarity of much contemporary American poetry — the reasons are complex and cannot be blamed solely on writing programs. I also do not believe that the limited audience for poetry is a recent phenomenon resulting from the 'irrelevant' or 'inaccessible' nature of contemporary writing — poetry has lacked a truly widespread audience since it stopped being communicated orally in a communal setting. It *is* true, however, that 1980's poetry in the United States is again dominated by an orthodoxy in the circles where money and prestige operate — in the pages of the *New Yorker,* in *Poetry,* or in the Washington offices of the National Endowment for the Arts, where decisions are made about who will receive writing grants.

Having painted a somewhat dismal view of 1980's mainstream American poetry — that it is less political or formally interesting than poetry of the 1960's and 70's — I now want to argue that there is innovative and powerful poetry being written in the United States. As in the 1950's, it is written on the margin of society and — it is unashamedly political, aggressive and passionate. June Jordan calls this marginalised writing 'New World' poetry, arguing that "there is an American, a New World, poetry that is as personal, as public, as irresistible, as quick, as necessary, as unprecedented, as representative, as exalted, as speakably commonplace, and as musical, as an emergency phone call". In describing 'New World' poets, Jordan is careful to be as inclusive as possible, emphasizing a shared attitude to experience and culture rather than attributes of class, race or gender allegiance: "Let me define my terms in brief: New World does not mean New England. New World means non-European; it means new, it means big, it means heterogenous, it means unknown, it means free, it means an end to feudalism, caste, privilege, and the violence of power. It means *wild* in the sense that a tree growing away from the earth enacts a wild event. It means *democratic* . . . ".[11]

It is too early to know if the 1980's brand of political poetry — whether termed 'New World' poetry or given another name — will overcome the obstacles facing all political poetry: the seductions of abstraction and simplification, the need to separate propaganda from art, and the difficulty of using the most popular contemporary form, the personal lyric, to address complex public issues. I am not arguing that 1980's political poetry is without its own flaws: over-reliance on narrative, a sometimes simplistic argumentation, occasional monotony of form and language. But I do believe that this poetry is mounting a serious and liberating challenge to orthodox assumptions about the form, content and purpose of poetry. Like Whitman's writing, it has crude moments; but also like Whitman's, it is the most invigorating and refreshing work of its period. In poems such as 'Second Poem from Nicaragua Libre: War Zone', June Jordan shows how one can avoid superficial rhetoric while exploring complex, politically-charged material, in this case the texture of life dominated by violence and fear of violence in Nicaragua:

> On the night road from El Rama the cows
> congregate full in the middle and you wait
> looking at the cowhide colors bleached
> by the high stars above their bodies
> big with ribs
>
> At some point you just have to trust
> somebody else the soldier
> wearing a white shirt the poet
> wearing glasses the woman
> wearing red shoes
> into combat

At dawn the student gave me a caramel
candy and pigs and dogs ran into the streets
as the sky began the gradual
wide burn and towards the top
of a new mountain I saw
the teen-age shadows of two sentries
armed with automatics
checking the horizon
for slow stars

American poetry — like American culture — has seen a myriad of cultural revolutions and counter-revolutions since 1900, with groups on the margin — such as Pound and Williams, or Ginsberg and Snyder — creating a radical poetics which eventually, after overcoming stubborn resistance, moved to the center. Ginsberg's 1986 reading at the Modern Language Association conference in New York — a conference comprised of academics who fifteen years ago would not have taught a word of *Howl* — shows his own emergence as an established poet. In 1984, Harper & Row acknowledged Ginsberg's status by bringing out his *Collected Poems*, becoming the first major publishing company to handle a Ginsberg book.

Given the breakthroughs achieved by American poets of the 1950's and 60's and the continuing urgency of political and cultural issues in the 1980's, it should not be surprising that the writing most likely to shape contemporary American poetry over the next decade is being written by poets speaking for those who live and/or write on society's margin. The work of Gwendolyn Brooks, Adrienne Rich, Audrey Lorde, and June Jordan challenges basic, orthodox assumptions about the nature of poetry and the structure of American society. I have named four women to reflect the fact that a great number of the controversial and influential poets of the 1980's are women battling the same kind of resistance that faced earlier American writers of politically and socially committed poetry. The best of these poets avoid rhetoric and theatricality in their search for an honest language and honest relations with the world they live in:

... we're not performers, like Liszt, competing
against the world for speed and brilliance
(the 79-year old pianist said, when I asked her
What makes a virtuoso? — Competitiveness.)
The longer I live the more I mistrust
theatricality, the false glamour cast
by performance, the more I know its poverty beside
the truths we are salvaging from
the splitting-open of our lives.

(from 'Transcendental Etude', by Adrienne Rich)[12]

Notes

1. By using "American" to refer to the United States for reasons of convenience, I do not mean to slight Canadian or South American poetry.
2. *International Directory of Little Magazines and Small Presses,* 23rd edition, Len Fulton and Ellen Ferber, eds. (Paradise, CA:Dustbooks, 1988): 766-774.
3. 'Poetic Injustice', *The New York Times Magazine* (May 29, 1988): 22.
4. The first phrase is T.S. Eliot's; the second, Seamus Heaney's. Heaney notes that he learned about the political dimension of poetry from his stay in Berkeley, California and resulting contact with the work of American poets such as Gary Snyder and Robert Bly. James Randall, 'An Interview with Seamus Heaney', *Ploughshares* 5.3 (1979): 20.
5. An exception is novelist Jack Kerouac, who was given to expressing right-wing nationalist opinions in the years before his death. See Ann Charters, *Kerouac* (San Francisco: Straight Arrow Books, 1973): 365.
6. *Time Magazine* particularly enjoyed baiting the 'Beats' during the 1950's.
7. I say "re-introduced" because June Jordan points out that Whitman was the American poet who first included direct political and social commentary in poetry. 'Preface' to *Passion* (Boston: Beacon Press, 1980): ix.
8. *Our Last First Poets: Vison and History in Contemporary American Poetry.* (Chicago: University of Illinois Press, 1981): ix.
9. Altieri, *Enlarging the Temple* (New Jersey: Associated University Presses, 1979): 226. See chapter 2 for a discussion of immanentist poetics.
10. Altieri 20.
11. *Passion.* Boston: Beacon Press, 1980: xi and xix.
12. *The Dream of a Common Language* (New York: W.W. Norton and Co., 1978).

ANTHONY CONRAN

Landscape With Moon, 1960

I.M. Victor Neep, d. 1979.

1.

As a churchyard has peace, because
In that place alone death has no power,

So to this territory of castles
— Dormant or extinct volcanoes of militarism —

Came one Neep, fugitive. From the deep
Arrow-slits his paintings look out.

2.

As a churchyard has peace, because
In that place alone profit is powerless,

So to this country of waste-tips
A whole industrial revolution away from him

Already melding into the mountains, with a working-class
Crafty and demoralised and picturesque,

And an ignorant Taffia holding off ruin with one hand
And with the other making sure of its getaway —

Came, in due season, Neep. He centred us.
His cottage was the hub of North Wales.

Bethesda, Caernarfon, Rhosgadfan. Metropolitan
Of painters, poets, dramatists

In the two languages. They were extraordinary times.
And we who are thrown by the wheel's force

Into the darkness, like sparks from a forge
— All of us — confess that fire, that hub rotating

And confess the stillness there, the watching
Crouched by an arrow-slit, for the moon.

TIM LIARDET

Palimpsest For A Radio Play

Wetherton polishes the Captain's forty spoons.
He replaces them in velvet casts like snug instruments.

He lays out the crumpled dog-rose in *The Oxford English*
And bemoans the Daimler's savage lacework of rust.

Baggage without handles! Without help Wetherton
Must keep the pains and visions from the older man's head

Like the voracious rats from the strawberry nets
Or bluebottles from kidneys staining the scrubbed table.

He has led the Captain back, confused and pathological,
Muttering bastardized verse with mud up to his knees;

He has heard his piss clattering on the foliage
Of the crepuscular alders, making his voice strange:

Cover her face, she died young; perfection is far away.
I shall sleep all night in my leaking galoshes.

The dusty-glassed lodge house, twenty years from India,
Swims in the chiaroscuro of its sycamore:

Their dependence externalises in a shabby order;
They bear each other's muted contusions with

246

An oblique if sacrosanct refusal to comment at all;
The magazines fade on the sill with the dead flies;

The broken ball-cock has been broken for a year;
It is the order of the lawn before the moles push up.

Into the other side of the lodge (it astrides the Gate)
Two spinsters assumed to be sisters move suddenly in:

Efficient in unpacking, alike, they sustain an air
Of determined insouciance, swinging their cello-cases.

The glow of an alien taste illumines isolation:
The small hours lap the little weights in their hems.

Wetherton sees one night the newly hung curtain draw back
And a pale blur of flesh dip at the steamy glass.

He fancies that he sees one patient sister yielding to
The other's comb, and hearing drifts of a soft adagio,

Peeps to see the two of them sitting naked with
Their cellos between their knees, their unravelled hair

Falling where they stoop to the sawing of their bows,
Long fingers active on the elongated strings.

Through a gin-obtuseness and the Captain's ear-hair
The image is conveyed, still cold from the night air.

Invited to tea, the women say little, exchanging looks,
Treated with the same degree of stilted attention

As were the barley field's shocked copulating couple
To whom the Captain raised his hat, as they covered up.

A corridor of trunks, discardments — no-man's-land —
Links the two men to the two women over the Gate.

In the camera obscura their movements are monitored.
Wetherton begins to relish, too much for self-esteem,

The weekly execution of the remonstrating hen
In an explosion of feathers. The strike from nowhere —

A storm over gravid wheat, breaking in the mind —
Leaves his right side as useless as the latest hen's:

This coincides with the sudden moving out of the women.
The deep vibrato of tensed springs at twilight

Is replaced by the usual background of estate crows.
It is as if, so to speak, the women were never there.

The Captain brings some warm eggs to the wheelchair
And lifts the little cosies: *voilà:* and taps spoon on shell.

And on a summer evening of deepening silences
That enter the upper room with the scent of mown hay

He unfolds the cloth and painstakingly identifies
The specimens, pinned out and helpless, under the glass.

After forty years of squeaking the glass Wetherton
Perceives the pins. He begins to wear the Captain's

Admittedly tatty and oversized plimsolls. His voice changes:
Cover her face, cover her face, cover her face.

HILARY LLEWELLYN-WILLIAMS

Breakfast With The Poets

Dawn at the Alcazaba. The poets come
up from the drowsy city, appearing like birds
from a woven nest of alleys
some walking, most in cars
turning difficult corners in the dark
all drawn to the honey rock

in scores, in hundreds
from under stones, on a breeze from the desert,
the folds of the sea. They've come
with spouses, friends and children, greeting
each other on the steps of the citadel
of light. That woman in evening dress
hasn't slept all night. That child,
like ours, stares through us,
eyes blank with dreams. They climb
and we climb with them
through the sultan's exquisite garden
shaping word after word.

Up in the high courtyard
are men with microphones, women
trailing long veils. Everyone laughs, delighted.
We lean together over rose-coloured walls,
watch the sun rise over ruined terraces.
This is a strange country
breeding poets instead of flies. They swarm
in the pure, steady light.

They hand out dazzling blankets:
like loaves and fishes, it's a miracle —
everyone sits down. Music swells
in a wild, muezzin cry.
A woman lifts brown arms, releasing

a pigeon. *See, I have laid*
my greeting in the collar of a dove
which will fly over the land
of Almería like a flung censer.

The poets read in turn
women and men, intensely
darkly and gloriously. Children wriggle:
I can't understand
all the words either; but they seem
poems of celebration.

Morning expands and blazes; the sun hits
the wall above us with a gold fist.
The city is awake: it roars
and glitters in wilderness; a bucket
of whitewash thrown at the mountains.
Comrade poets, ladies, gentlemen,
now breakfast will be served:
herb tea and spicecakes in the high tower
of Ibn Al-Mu'tasim.

(Note: *See, I have laid my greeting* . . . from a poem by Al-Mu'tasim Ibn
Sumadih, Prince of Almería in the 11th century AD.)

AUTHOR AND VOLUME INDEX

R. George Thomas
  Dylan Thomas And Some Early Readers (Prose) [Vol. 9.2, 1973] 94

R.S. Thomas
  Loyalties (Vol. 4.1, 1968) 33
  Chat (Vol. 7.1, 1971) 60
  Feminine Gender (Vol. 18.3, 1982) 176

John Tripp
  Elegy For Jack Jones (Vol. 6.4, 1971) 59

John Powell Ward
  Here, Home (Vol. 10.4, 1975) 116
  Editorial (Vol. 13.1, 1977) 129

Vernon Watkins
  Swallows (Vol. 3.1, 1967) 17

Harri Webb
  Thanks In Winter (Vol. 3.1, 1967) 16
  Cywydd (Vol. 5.2, 1969) 46

Nigel Wells
  Y Plygaint (Vol. 13.2, 1977) 136

Frances Williams
  Siesta Time (Vol. 21.4, 1986) 210

Gwyn Williams
  Skull Of The World, Cadbury Hill (Vol. 6.3, 1970) 57

Herbert Williams
  Depopulation (Vol. 1.1, 1965) 11

John Stuart Williams
  In Marienbad (Vol. 6.2, 1970) 49

Raymond Williams
  Excerpt From An Interview (Vol. 13.3, 1977) 138

Rhydwen Williams
  A Letter To The Editor (Vol. 8.2, 1972) 80

.